THE TEACHER TOOLKIT GUIDE TO FEEDBACK

PRAISE FOR THE TEACHER TOOLKIT GUIDE TO FEEDBACK

'In a period where we are searching "AI" and Ed Tech for workload solutions, Ross reminds us of the fundamental importance of pellucid high-quality reciprocal feedback between teacher and learner. The evidence base is compelling; the practical application is explained clearly by colleagues in case studies working with children and young people every day. Another fantastic contribution to the conversation on pedagogy and best practice. Well done and thank you Teacher Toolkit!'

Tom Campbell, CEO, EACT

'*The Teacher Toolkit Guide to Feedback* offers educators an opportunity to leverage existing practices by refining and maximising the potential of formative assessments. Rather than suggesting we learn yet another new strategy, as others often do, Ross helps educators build on existing knowledge. What a refreshing way to improve the craft of teaching.'

Sarah Oberle, teacher and EdD candidate

'Ross has a real knack for simplifying reams of complicated research to produce clear, actionable ideas for the classroom. His aim is to transform how students receive and implement feedback, but importantly, he has teacher wellbeing as well as efficacy at the heart of it all. This is certainly a book that all senior leaders should have on their reading list if they wish to make an important impact in these two areas.'

Jon Wayth, MEd, headteacher

'So often a major discussion point of parents, students and teachers, feedback can be a help or hindrance. Teacher Toolkit ensures that feedback is effective, accessible and manageable for all involved. This book is a must for all, from school leaders to those entering the profession.'

Glyn Potts MBE DL, headteacher, Newman College

‘Thoroughly researched, this is a superb primer for the world of feedback. Using provocations, thoughtful case studies and ideas you can implement, this latest book from Ross is an excellent guide for teachers and leaders.’

Stephen Lockyer, teacher and author

‘It is hard to get into other schools to see fantastic ideas and practice, but this book uses relevant school case studies to highlight great new ideas and practice, of which all have a huge impact directly related to teachers in the classroom and student progress. An incredibly useful toolbox of ideas to be used as a hub of any school CPD session.’

Libby Isaac, deputy headteacher, Kingfisher Schools Trust

‘What sets this book apart is the way Ross McGill is really clear about all types of formative assessment and how they can be used at appropriate times in different settings. The book brings together a huge range of research evidence as well as the culmination of Ross’s own practice and experiences. It is very easy to navigate and should be at every teacher’s side!’

Tracey O’Brien, author and headteacher

‘This publication is a real blend of theory and practice, coupled with real-world classroom examples. It makes this book an essential read for teachers looking to refine their feedback techniques. The clear models and detailed explanations empower educators to deliver feedback that truly enhances student learning and development.’

Helen Young, head of teaching, learning, assessment and innovation at St Helens and Knowsley Community College

‘I cannot recommend this book enough. For any schools, leaders or teachers looking to improve the way they give feedback AND reduce staff workload, this book is an absolute goldmine of methods and practical applications.’

Sarah Larsen, teacher

‘This book is a treasure trove of practical advice and innovative strategies. It is an indispensable tool for educators. It’s like having a mentor at your fingertips!’

George Walker, teacher of computer science, Moor Park High School and Sixth Form, Preston

BLOOMSBURY EDUCATION
Bloomsbury Publishing Plc
50 Bedford Square, London, WC1B 3DP, UK
29 Earlsfort Terrace, Dublin 2, Ireland

BLOOMSBURY, BLOOMSBURY EDUCATION and the Diana logo are trademarks of Bloomsbury Publishing Plc

First published in Great Britain, 2024

This edition published in Great Britain 2024 by Bloomsbury Publishing Plc

A catalogue record for this book is available from the British Library

ISBN: PB: 978-1-8019-9525-2; ePDF: 978-1-8019-9534-4; ePub: 978-1-8019-9535-1

2 4 6 8 10 9 7 5 3 (paperback)

Text design by Marcus Duck Design

Printed and bound in the UK by CPI Group Ltd, CR0 4YY

To find out more about our authors and books visit www.bloomsbury.com and sign up for our newsletters

THE TEACHER TOOLKIT GUIDE TO FEEDBACK

ROSS MORRISON McGILL

BLOOMSBURY EDUCATION
LONDON OXFORD NEW YORK NEW DELHI SYDNEY

CONTENTS

ACKNOWLEDGEMENTS

This book represents the culmination of seven years of thinking and experiences. The catalyst for me? A clumsy inspection process that rigidly adhered to written policies, overlooking the nuanced efforts of our expert teachers. This paradigm, where written marking is king, inspired me to challenge the quality assurance processes used for inspection and question the efficacy of written feedback in our schools and colleges, especially for observations and work scrutiny.

The Verbal Feedback Project (2019) research with **Mark Quinn**, commissioned by University College London, was a significant milestone in this book's journey.

This book has been a joy to publish, thanks to brilliant contributions from nine schools and colleges. Thank you to **Helen Nelson** and **Sara Scott** (Joseph Cash Primary School, Chapter 1 contributors), **Rosetta Dyer** and **Anouska Sehmi** (Dollis Primary School, Ch. 2), **Hailee McAuley, Darren Gallagher, Satnam Dosanjh** and **Umar Malik** (Waverley School, Ch. 3), **Ryan Curran** and **Paul Hillary** (Delta Independent School, Ch. 4), **Tim Waldron** (Everton Free School, Ch. 5), **Sam Martin** (Kennet School, Ch. 6), **Esther Suttle** and **Sarah Haslam** (Withington Girls' School, Ch. 7), **James Hinton** and **Alan Thomson** (Leaways School, Ch. 8) and **Sabeena Shah, Christina Morris, Jolanta Wlodek** and **Marina Clark** (West London College, Ch. 9).

Thank you to **Emily Evans** and to **Susannah Fountain** for their support, patience and encouragement along the way, fact-checking, questioning and challenging my contributions to reshape the material into something coherent and comprehensible. Thanks also to **Elaine Tuffery** for a sterling job in bringing all the content together! This book was inspired by the research of **Prof John Hattie** and **Prof Rob Coe**, so I am especially grateful to John for his contributions.

Finally, as always, thank you to my family, **Jenni** and **Freddie**, for putting up with me through all the highs and lows!

Scan to listen to a short welcome message I have recorded for you

FOREWORD

I took courses at university in the 1960s when behaviourism was still dominant, and feedback was a major topic. Since then, there has been a revolution in our understanding about feedback, yet it remains central to most theories of learning. A pivotal moment in this evolution was the publication of an article by Kluger and DeNisi in 1996, which significantly reshaped how we view the relationship between feedback and performance. Their meta-analysis revealed that while feedback interventions generally increased learning (with an effect size of d = .41), about one-third of these interventions actually decreased learning. This variability has become a core concept, driving extensive research into understanding when and where feedback is effective and when it is not.

Kluger and DeNisi demonstrated that feedback affects attention allocation, influencing task learning, task motivation and meta-tasks (such as self-related aspects). They found that the effectiveness of feedback interventions diminishes as attention shifts from the task itself to the self. Numerous studies, including our own, have since built upon their pioneering work to elucidate the dynamics of feedback, aiming to provide a nuanced understanding of how feedback operates and to avoid the oversimplified notion that 'more feedback' is always beneficial.

We have extended this work by proposing three key questions (Where am I going? How am I going? Where to next?) and identifying four levels of feedback: task, process, self-regulation and self. Ross McGill uses these three questions as a foundation throughout his book. He interprets the first question, 'Where am I going?' as 'feed-up', which involves comparing a student's current status with the target status, necessitating teachers making success criteria explicit. The second question, 'How am I going?' corresponds to 'feedback', which compares current performance with past performance; our experiences and McGill's case studies show that teachers excel in providing this type of feedback. The third question, 'Where to next?' translates to 'feed-forward', which involves explaining the target status and providing guidance on the next steps students should take to achieve success.

Our surveys indicate that teachers tend to focus on the first two questions, dedicating most of their resources to these areas. In contrast, students are particularly interested in the third question, as they are keen to know how to improve (they are 'improvement engines'). In one study, we provided two pages of feedback to junior high students, half of which included 'Where to next?' or feed-forward feedback, while the other half did not. Students who did not receive feed-forward feedback claimed they received 'no' feedback at all. This underscores the importance of feed-forward feedback, which also relies on the credibility provided by feed-up and feed-back comments. As Ross McGill notes, 'Feedback must be delivered so that a student can act upon the recommendations.'

This insight led us to explore how students hear, listen to and act upon feedback. We discovered that feedback often entails costs (e.g. having to redo work), making it easier for students to engage in selective listening and ignore feedback. Therefore, we suggest that effective feedback is that which is heard, understood and acted upon. Kluger and DeNisi's finding that one-third of feedback interventions decrease performance could be expanded to include feedback that does not impact learning because it is not heard, understood or acted upon.

This book delves into each of the three feedback questions and examines the written, verbal and non-verbal forms of feedback. I have little time for the argument that written feedback is inherently better or worse than verbal feedback, that grades are superior or inferior to comments, or that positive feedback is more effective than negative feedback. The key is the content of the feedback and its ability to be heard, understood and acted upon by the recipient. Thus, all three forms (written, verbal and non-verbal) across the three feedback questions are critical. This comprehensive approach is the major contribution of this book. This is indeed an important book and I am honoured to play a little part in it.

Professor John Hattie
University of Melbourne

INTRODUCTION: THE DIALOGUE AROUND MARKING AND FEEDBACK

The dialogue around marking across English education has shifted dramatically. Due to various market forces, teachers may be told to mark once a week or use a specific-coloured pen. While this thinking has some merit in specific contexts, I want to explain why I have written *The Teacher Toolkit Guide to Feedback* and share with you my present-day thinking and how it may inspire you and the next generation of teachers to help move the profession forward.

The first thing to declare is that this is **NOT** just a book about feedback. It's a book about **all** forms of formative assessment in the classroom, covering a range of in-class and out-of-class strategies.

The root meaning of 'assessment'

Have you ever considered the etymological meaning of the word 'assessment'? I discovered its origins about five years ago and I wish it had been made more explicit in my teacher training. The word 'assess' derives from the Latin '*assidere*', which means 'to sit beside'. Therefore, 'to assess means to sit beside the learner' (Stefanakis, 2002, p. 9).

The challenge for all of us, of course, is that you cannot sit beside all students in every lesson. It's impossible! So, how do you use this meaning to change your perspective? In our evolution as teachers, we learn that assessment can be summative or formative. It takes us several years to understand how both types manifest themselves in our classroom. When we factor in different age groups, subject disciplines, time pressures and external demands, it is not surprising to see why we may develop a blurred understanding of assessment! Let me provide you with a formal definition of summative and formative assessment, followed by my teacher-friendly take on these.

- **Formative assessment:** To monitor student learning using informal means and to provide meaningful feedback to students to support them to take action.
- **Summative assessment:** To evaluate student learning with a formal in-class or end-of-term assessment. A grade is provided to report back to the student on their efforts.

Now, my interpretation to help teachers:

- **Formative:** To share informal feedback with the student about their journey so far.
- **Summative:** To summarise an end-point with a grade (sum).

Marking and feedback across English schools and colleges

Over the last two decades, we have experienced increasing accountability pressures across England. This means having any time to 'sit beside' a student has been eroded. Instead, we spend a lot of time providing numbers and grades on a computer screen and marking or carrying our students' books from the classroom to our kitchen table at home, sitting alone to assess the work.

We have clearly lost our way, and the profession should reconsider workload and accountability demands in light of reduced funding. This is in spite of a requirement to maintain the same standards, combined with a dwindling workforce and increasing recruitment pressures. It's simply not possible for teachers to work in the same way and we must rethink our approach.

The aim of this book is to question everything we know about evaluating assessment in the classroom to help keep as many of us as possible in the profession.

As we navigate through the book, I will introduce **nine formative assessment concepts** to inspire your classroom. My aim is that it will change the way you view 'marking' and 'feedback' **forever**! In each chapter, I will share a case study from an English school or college, showcasing their work in a particular area. A range of contexts and locations are represented – each school is shown on the map below.

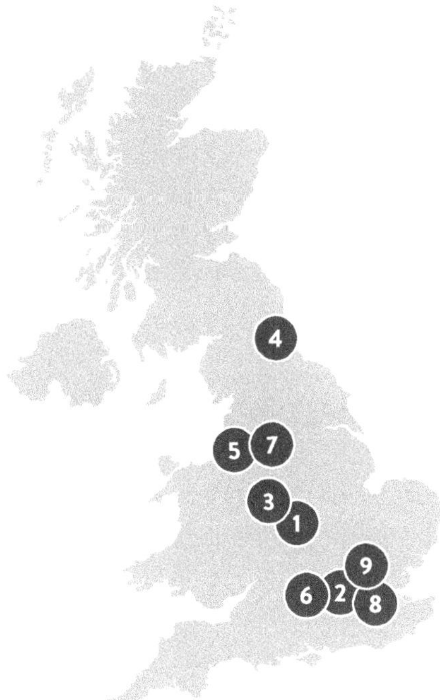

Case Study Chapters

1. Joseph Cash Primary School: Coventry
2. Dollis Primary School: North London
3. Waverley School: Birmingham
4. Delta Independent School: County Durham
5. Everton Free School: Liverpool
6. Kennet School: Berkshire
7. Withington Girls' School: Manchester
8. Leaways School: East London
9. West London College: West London

Understanding the historical context of formative assessment across the English education system will help when considering alternative ways of working and acknowledging the impact of policies, pedagogical trends and assessment frameworks.

While I believe all schools and colleges are doing one or two aspects from each of the nine chapters, very few are promoting **all** nine methods in their teaching and learning policies, and even fewer of these organisations can articulate how they evidence each method (by outcomes) in their quality control and assurance procedures.

Influences on marking and feedback

There are two influences on internal 'marking' procedures in our institutions. The first influence is the methods that the leadership team chooses for internal 'marking and feedback'. The second influence is the pressures outside of the classroom – for example, inspections, parents and examinations – that coerce you into providing written evidence for external verification. This consequence is very separate from the former, yet often stifles the organic decisions made internally, sending you into a marking frenzy, where any chosen method becomes not a process for the student, but a way of justifying all the work completed. This evidence trail for inspectors offers a documented journey of progress for somebody else not sitting beside the student, to make an obscure link to impact on teaching quality. This shift from pedagogy towards an unsustainable level of accountability needs a U-turn.

Only a decade or so ago, marking was viewed largely as a summative process – a mechanism to evaluate student performance, with teachers doing most of the work. However, today, despite the rhetoric evolving to a place where 'live assessment' is the preferred approach, marking is still reported as the number one burden for teachers, taking up 'too much time' (DfE, 2023a, p. 15).

The seminal work of *Inside the Black Box* (Black and Wiliam, 1998a) did offer some hope; wholesome approaches to formative feedback began to gain some traction, promising to enhance student achievement. This dialogue influenced the national standards and external metrics of its time, with a shift towards empowering teachers and their pedagogical approaches, notably formative assessment in the classroom. This made a difference not just to the piece of work, but on the students themselves and on individual performance as a whole. The central message was that the student should be working harder than you, and that it wasn't just about what feedback you provided, but how the student acted upon that assessment.

However, there is still an underlying assumption that providing effective feedback requires marking policies to stipulate how every teacher across the school should assess. This desire for consistency is unsustainable and unrealistic, significantly increasing your workload.

One influence? It started in 1992, when a well-known inspectorate once viewed 'marking policies' and 'feedback techniques' as a measure of teaching quality. In-class assessment has since evolved towards more refined approaches that add value and impact. However, in classrooms up and down the country, providing effective feedback has meant unsustainable working hours, while marking books or leaving verbal feedback stamps has a negligible impact on students.

The inspectorate intensified a culture of excessive marking, with triple-marking and endless marking codes becoming the tipping point.

Quality assurance procedures meant that when you marked a student's book, you needed to provide evidence that a consistent approach had been used between classrooms, and that the student had responded with a comment or an improvement in their work based on your feedback. To make matters worse, you were then expected to reply to this response once more! The consequence? Endless loops of assessment on one piece of classwork.

Not many people know that, according to Department for Education (DfE) data, the average career span of a teacher in England is just 13 years (DfE, 2023a)! We know that 'marking' impacts all of you, regardless of the age group you teach or the type of school you work in.

The individual preferences of inspectors have now evolved to empower schools to make their own decisions on how to mark. This stance was taken after the teaching profession questioned the inspectorate's research reliability. However, we still have work to do!

Misconceptions about other types of formative assessment, especially how they can be evaluated, are still widespread. For example, the quantity of feedback exceeds the quality provided, with copious amounts of marking as a good measure of pedagogical diligence. This can easily be perpetuated by school leaders, who value some teachers' contributions as a model of excellence, when clearly someone may be working every hour of the day and night. Show me a teacher who uses various teaching ideas and gets the job done effectively during the school day!

All of this contradicts the research on effective teaching – for example 'The power of feedback' (Hattie and Timperley, 2007) – and any influences on formative assessment. The rise in accountability measures and performance across England means our schools prioritise some parts of curriculum content over others. This scrutiny also impacts our pedagogical choices. Any dissonance between research and practice reminds us that 'implementation science' – the process of adopting approaches found to be effective by research in teaching practices – can be a long one. There is therefore an urgent need for teacher professional development that bridges the gap between robust evidence and myths that continue to hold the profession back.

It became clear to me many years ago that marking and feedback systems were brutal, penalising teachers for their goodwill and professionalism. You would hope we are in a better place as we move into the next decade. Delving into academic research, I wanted to question the status quo further, exploring evidence-informed alternatives to help resolve some of these issues.

The Education Endowment Foundation's 'A marked improvement' (Elliott et al., 2016) provided further evidence and a nuanced understanding of formative assessment that resonated with many of you. Then the DfE's 'School workload reduction toolkit' (DfE, 2018) offered some alternative ways forward, with guidance updated in an online toolkit of resources to 'Improve workload and wellbeing for school staff' (DfE, 2024).

When I met John Hattie on a shared keynote stage in 2017, I didn't know I had already started my academic journey with education research. What is now inside this book is something I could not articulate back then. I had only really considered written or verbal feedback in my pedagogy.

Hattie's seminal research *Visible Learning* (2009) heavily influenced the teaching profession, redefining our appreciation of the power of feedback and its application. Key phrases such as 'manageable', 'meaningful and motivational' and 'timely' began to ripple across the profession and appeared in countless school and college teaching and learning policies. Teachers began to understand that feedback was a high-impact strategy and to question extensive written commentary in student books. It essentially killed off 'triple-marking'. Hattie's work continues to inspire tens of thousands of you worldwide.

Research by Professor Rob Coe, 'Improving education: A triumph of hope over experience' took my thinking one step further, challenging teachers to rethink inefficient marking policies that required high effort for low impact. 'We invest massive effort and cost in implementing new ideas, and it is likely that some of them bring genuine improvement. However, it is also likely that some – perhaps just as many – lead to deterioration.' (Coe, 2013, p. xvi)

The era of workload and new ways of effective working was developing, questioning the reliability and validity of any classroom approach. Delving deeper into Coe's work, I read further research:

- 'Learning versus performance: An integrative view' (Soderstrom and Bjork, 2015)
- 'Can feedback improve teaching?' (Coe, 2006).

Both are very important pieces of research for anyone deeply interested in feedback.

Soderstrom and Bjork (2015) considered what we can observe and measure as performance – but also that this is often an unreliable indicator of whether any long-term changes have taken place in memory. Developing knowledge requires conscious effort and deliberate practice, and raises further questions about traditional methods of marking and feedback. Is extensive written feedback, for example, worth the effort? Does 'tick and flick' add any value? Do verbal feedback stamps help students recall the actual conversation in the future?

Imagine the scenario: I mark your essay, which is a high grade, but I decide to delay the feedback as you have a big exam next week and I don't want you to become over-confident too early, so delaying the good news keeps you working to the finishing line. The 'timing' of how feedback is received is important, and from my work with schools across the country, features heavily in many teaching and learning policies.

Very few schools have considered many of the **conditions that impact formative assessment** – what Coe calls 'influences' – which help them to understand how their approaches to formative assessment can lead to new ways of providing marking and feedback and, more importantly, how to evidence teacher impact on student outcomes beyond traditional marking.

Scan to view different types of feedback influences

In 2019, I had the opportunity to conduct the 'Verbal Feedback Project Report' (McGill and Quinn, 2019) with funding from University College London (UCL) to empirically test alternatives to written marking, and to challenge the notion that the best way to provide feedback to students is to ensure that everything is written down. Conducted with seven state schools across England, the research trial concluded that there appears to be no detrimental impact on student outcomes.

The research considered past publications from the DfE and international examples, exploring formative assessment techniques that significantly reduced the burden of written comments required from teachers. Techniques included framing feedback in zonal areas of a student's work, using scripts to develop dialogic conversations with students, and encouraging 'eureka moments' where students take action, rather than rely on monologic commentary from the teacher, with a hit and, more likely, miss impact on the student. The ultimate nirvana was to provide evidence for schools and colleges to illustrate that moving towards more in-class formative methods reduced workload, provided immediate impact and, in particular, could be substantiated by a range of evidence across student outcomes.

Throughout the research, I began to understand and see for myself what effective feedback could and should look like from a group of teachers who were keen to develop an evidence base that was sensitive to teacher workload. We provided clear alternatives for schools and teachers to use in their teaching and learning policies. This blend of theory and practice shows that classroom-based research has significant value in shaping national policy and accountability processes that are influencing schools.

The COVID-19 pandemic and beyond

The dialogue for formative assessment in the classroom has changed over the last five years. The COVID-19 pandemic and the immediate switch to online learning (and marking) provided a period of disruption and evolution, with many online quizzes and software platforms providing immediate assessments for students to self-assess.

In-class, low-effort methods for teachers that give immediate feedback now offer high-impact solutions for students and are the preferred option for many schools. Some of these solutions provide research-informed decisions, rather than the outdated marking policies that see teachers voting with their feet and opting to work in other schools or elsewhere. In cutting-edge schools, school leaders are innovative, sensitive to teacher wellbeing and workload, and research-rich about which methods provide more 'bang for your buck'! Schools that continue to promote 'marking once a week' policies, chasing specific procedures in half-termly work scrutiny to appease inspections, will soon see themselves looking around and asking, 'Where have all our teachers gone?'

I know change is not universal, and in my work with hundreds of schools across the country, selected methods must be contextualised. For example, students from disadvantaged backgrounds, those with special educational needs or younger pupils with developing cognitive abilities will need a mixed approach to assessment. In this context, these decisions must be protected and valued as the right tool for the job, rather than accountability getting in the way of the preferred methods chosen in specific circumstances.

In my book, *The Teacher Toolkit Guide to Questioning* (McGill, 2023), I explore how questioning could improve performance through scripts and dialogic techniques, which are other branches of formative assessment we often do not associate with marking and feedback. These provide immediate methods for students to respond, but can be difficult to quality-assure.

The need for change

The evidence is clear. The more challenging the school context, the more likely that you are required to assess in particular ways to ensure students make progress. While this is an obvious and desirable approach, it comes with some of the consequences discussed earlier. A small dose of accountability enables everyone to work to a 'hymn sheet', ensuring standards are met and goals are clearly communicated.

However, my aim is that we should consider new ways of thinking about formative assessment in the classroom. What techniques can be used? Importantly, how can these techniques be monitored and evaluated by leaders and inspectors? Marking has been, for too long, an exhausting one-way street that now needs to be supported by other classroom techniques.

Drawing upon observations across 500+ schools, I can conclude that, as teachers, you do not need **consistency**. Consistency sometimes manifests itself as stringent compliance, impacting on your mental health, salary and sometimes your career! No school I've ever visited has claimed to have achieved 100 per cent consistency in, for example, teaching and learning, so why should we continue to desire something that is unobtainable? Every school **wants** consistency, but do they **need** it? More importantly, if they need consistency between classrooms, do they ever achieve it? It's my evidence-based belief that they do not.

What teachers want is **coherence**. Many teachers would like to have an active say in school policy design, where excellent school leadership brings people together to talk about complex school problems. The result? Innovative school policies that balance teacher autonomy and accountability, providing everyone with a degree of autonomy. Professional development sessions encourage you to bring along a giant pile of 'unmarked' classroom books and ask, 'How would you assess these books in 15 minutes?' This is the type of school culture you need and want. This type of school culture ensures that you are free to ask supportive and challenging questions to ensure standards are met and are always being developed. It is a space in which you can discuss, share and employ evidence-based practices.

This evolution of thought took another significant step for me. In 'The power of feedback' (2007), Hattie and Timperley argued 'that feedback cannot be understood as a single consistent form of treatment' and that feedback can have different perspectives:

1. 'feed-up' (comparison of the actual status with a target status
2. 'feedback' (comparison of the actual status with a previous status
3. 'feed-forward' (explanation of the target status based on the actual status).

This is where an enormous light bulb lit up in my head!

What if I expanded on written, verbal and non-verbal feedback? What would happen if I searched for examples of how feed-up, feedback and feed-forward appeared in our classrooms, and how they improved student outcomes? **This was how the concept for this book was born!**

A better understanding of formative assessment

In conclusion, if we want to better support our teachers from burnout and excessive quality assurance processes, or help students who are frustrated with the feedback they receive, we must move towards a deeper understanding of formative assessment. There has already been some significant work completed in this field, but what I see on the ground is schools are limited by their understanding, the nuances of their feedback and how they can demonstrate the methods they choose in direct correlation to student outcomes. Again, we should challenge the notion that written feedback is the only way to evidence how students make progress.

What if schools and colleges were more confident, evidencing verbal feedback in students' outcomes, providing clear evidence of how conversations conducted by you in your classrooms (not seen by observers, inspectors or parents) clearly impact student progress? And without gimmicks such as the verbal feedback stamps! What if the non-verbal gestures, all those everyday 'thumbs up' and 'smiles' and 'reassuring nods' to the shy student sitting at the other side of the classroom, clearly made a difference to exam grades, attendance or engagement in class?

What if schools and colleges knew how to use all of these techniques more explicitly in their practice? What if our inspectors had a better understanding of evaluating formative assessment? What if we all had a broader view of the evidence, particularly the methods used that cannot be seen in students' exercise books or in final pieces of coursework? Wouldn't our profession be in a better place?

In this book, I present nine different techniques that **teachers are already using**. The schools and college case studies, and their ideas within each chapter, represent a deeper perspective on what feedback and marking could look like if we can help shift the current narrow view evident in some areas of the sector. These nine key themes are:

1. written feedback
2. written feed-up
3. written feed-forward
4. verbal feedback
5. verbal feed-up
6. verbal feed-forward
7. non-verbal feedback
8. non-verbal feed-up
9. non-verbal feed-forward.

The above text summarises my thinking over the last decade: a vision of a more nuanced future for marking and feedback – nine forms of formative assessment for the classroom, where each has value. Even if your *current* quality assurance processes cannot evidence them, this book should help your understanding and delivery of formative assessment.

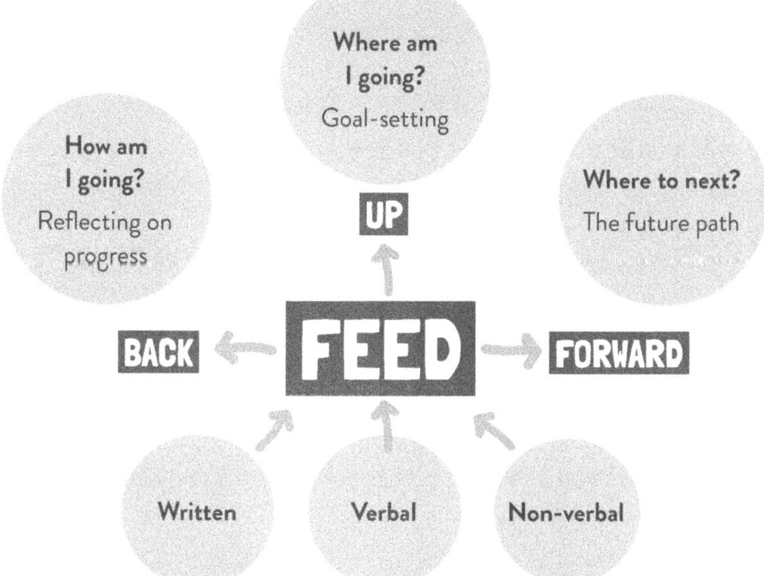

Schools and colleges can develop a deeper understanding of marking and feedback by aligning any understanding of formative assessment with direct empirical evidence. I write this message specifically for school or college leaders and inspectors, who can do better with the quality control and quality assurance processes evaluated in our classrooms.

While I accept there are specific things teachers need to do for qualifications, away from the shining lights of the final examination, there is an opportunity for teachers and leaders to develop a more expansive repertoire of techniques to reduce the marking burden for all teachers and, at the same time, widen their understanding. We need a much more sustainable, refined and thoughtful approach to the brilliant and complex work that we all do in our classrooms. My aim is that this book will help give you a more nuanced view of formative assessment, and that this book becomes a major step forward in your journey.

Teachers engaging with research

Before social media platforms became popular, teachers largely had to rely on local authorities, libraries, unions, subject associations and their school leadership teams for information to develop their practice. Today, through the power of social media, teachers can control this continued professional development (CPD) for themselves, connecting with academics or teaching colleagues in other countries to develop evidence-informed practice. This is the real beauty of building networks and connections in order to remain curious about teaching and learning.

A recent email exchange between myself and educator John Hattie exemplifies the point. In it, there is a fabulous piece of insight from Hattie: that students may receive lots of feedback (How am I going?) or feed-up (Where am I going?), but if they do not believe they have any feed-forward (Where to next?), they can be left feeling that they don't know what to do!

Scan to view an email exchange highlighting the practice of social research

More importantly, without feed-forward, students will *not* perceive that their teacher has helped them, despite plenty of written or verbal feedback or feed-up! It is an important point.

2002

Stefanakis explores the etymology of 'assessment', i.e. 'to sit beside'.

2006

'Can feedback improve teaching?' by Prof Rob Coe is published. The phrases 'manageable', 'meaningful' and 'motivation' start to ripple across the profession.

2007

Hattie and Timperley publish 'The power of feedback', highlighting the impact of effective feedback on student outcomes.

2009

Visible Learning by John Hattie is published, reshaping the profession's view of feedback and its impact.

2013

'Improving education' by Prof Rob Coe is published, questioning the effectiveness of marking policies.

2015

'Learning vs. performance' by Soderstrom and Bjork is published, challenging observation.

2016

The Education Endowment Foundation (EEF) publishes 'A marked improvement' (Elliott et al., 2016).

2018

'School workload reduction toolkit' is published by the DfE, offering strategies to reduce teacher workload concerning marking and feedback. Written commentary on how schools approach marking and feedback is phased out in inspections.

2019

The Verbal Feedback Project is published by Ross and Mark Quinn (UCL), highlighting how seven disadvantaged state schools explored alternatives to written marking, achieving similar or better outcomes.

2020

Wisniewski et al. publish a new meta-analysis of empirical research, stating 'feedback cannot be understood as a single consistent form of treatment'. Clearly, only using the phrase 'feedback' is heavily outdated.

HOW TO USE THIS BOOK

What you'll find in each chapter

In this book, I will explore what I've been learning about marking and feedback and why I truly believe that understanding the efficacy behind marking and providing meaningful feedback for students will significantly influence how you teach.

As educators, we have important choices influencing how we can support (or hinder) the learning process. For example, how can you successfully implement different forms of assessment without the burden of triple-marking? I will introduce you to nine types of formative assessment based upon the concepts of 'feedback, feed-up and feed-forward' to help in your delivery of effective marking and dialogue with your students. In addition, I will introduce you to nine case studies from a variety of educational establishments that showcase best practice.

My key objective is to provide you with some initial theory that can then be turned into a practical activity for you to complete as you read through the book. This will help you to model the learning process as you move through the material.

Each chapter is divided into four key sections.

1. Explainer

The first part of each chapter covers **what you need to know** about the discussed topic and delves into the research on various feedback models. Explainers are supported by infographics and diagrams that will promote your understanding of these concepts.

2. Practical idea

After the explainer, we'll consider a practical idea that turns the **theory into practice**. Chapters 1 to 9 each include one case study school or college to demonstrate how teachers are using a range of formative assessments in the classroom. Each case study explains how the teachers are implementing the idea in practice, with recommendations and suggestions for how you might be able to apply the idea to best effect in your context.

At the end of the idea, you'll find a set of **toolkit tips**, which are practical takeaways to support you when putting the idea into practice in your classroom.

3. Worked example

I'll give you a **worked example** of how the practical idea could work in practice. I will aim to demonstrate how each chapter idea supports student progress, metacognition and action, following whatever form of formative assessment method is provided by the teacher.

4. Template

At the end of Chapters 1 to 9, a **template** is provided to help you plan how to implement the practical idea in your classroom. Use the template to make the idea relevant to your students and translate the concept into your context. When you're delivering the practical ideas or using the templates with your students, it's a good idea to name the technique you are using – for example, feedback, feed-up or feed-forward. This will help your students to identify each technique and enable them to learn how to respond and understand what is expected of them.

The templates are also available online, so you can download and print them. Scan the QR code next to each template for access.

Bringing it all together

In the final part of the book, I will show you how you can bring all the practical ideas together to support learning and progress across an academic year. I will suggest how you might embed the ideas into your curriculum, and how to implement the theory and practical ideas shared in the book. I will explain how you could lead teacher training sessions so the ideas complement and build on each other to maximise their impact on student outcomes.

CHAPTER 1

WRITTEN FEEDBACK

Written feedback can be defined as detailed reflective comments that look at previous performance and areas to develop.
(Feedback = How am I going?)

One of the most significant challenges for all teachers is managing the burden of marking, especially written feedback. Marking takes different forms, not only between subjects, but between age groups as well, from Early Years classrooms to secondary schools, and into further education.

Marking is often considered to be the number one method to deliver quality assurance and evaluation. This evaluation mutates into detailed marking codes. For example, triple-marking occurs when you assess the student's work, the student responds and then you are expected to respond to the student's second attempt! There may be specified ways of providing this written feedback, and you are held to account for 'one way or no way at all'. This can lead to significant teacher workload and worsening mental health.

The purpose of written commentary is to allow students to refer back to it later. As such, it is a vital aspect of formative assessment; the feedback you deliver to the student is designed to guide and improve the student's understanding, skills and subsequent performance. Therefore, written feedback, by definition, has to be recorded by you, either in or out of the lesson. Put simply, 'feedback' is reporting back on the progress of work reviewed in the past. Therefore, you (or the student, in some peer-assessment methods) evaluate the progress on the work made.

Feedback must be delivered so that a student can act upon the recommendations. As mentioned, this actionable feedback will look very different in an Early Years classroom from a further education context, and as you will discover as we progress through the book, the variations between subjects will also be considered and explored in more detail in due course.

While self-assessment (a student marking their own work based on criteria given by the teacher) and peer review (students marking each other's work) have their place, the teacher predominantly delivers written feedback because it carries the weight of professional expertise and knowledge and, hopefully, provides the impact that it needs. This written feedback should help students achieve the required expertise they need to progress; it will also reassure parents that their child is being given the necessary guidance to improve. A significant proportion of your workload is determining the best method for diagnosing how to correct the issues in students' work.

In this chapter and each subsequent chapter, I will introduce you to one case study school that provides an example of each of the nine formative assessment techniques outlined in the Introduction. The purpose is to help teachers use any or all of the methods promoted throughout this book, and for school and college leaders to consider how they can evaluate the strategy for quality assurance.

At the end of the chapter, you will consider how the strategies highlighted in each case study, including any academic evidence, may be applied in other educational settings where students' responses to assessment might vary significantly. You will also explore how written feedback can be structured to be clear, constructive and focused on specific aspects of students' work.

EXPLAINER

Some key theories behind writing feedback in the English primary school classroom originate from the process writing movement of the 1970s (Hardman and Bell, 2017). Teachers will be most familiar with assessment and classroom learning (Black and Wiliam, 1998b, p. 8): 'Feedback to students should focus on the task, should be given regularly and while still relevant, and should be specific to the task.'

Studies have shown that the quality of feedback was the largest influence on student performance, with feedback being the 'most effective, when it was designed to stimulate correction of errors through a thoughtful approach' to the original learning (Black and Wiliam, 1998b, p. 36).

In another interesting piece of research, 'More fronted adverbials than ever before', Hardman and Bell (2017) provide examples of written feedback, practice and grammatical metalanguage from three classrooms in an English primary school. The findings suggest that despite good feedback and a good understanding of grammar between teachers and children, feedback was often provided at the surface level, focused on the mechanical or technical aspects of grammar, such as punctuation and layout, rather than deeper content-related aspects. In direct corrections, the teacher corrected the writing and in indirect corrections the 'error' was highlighted by symbols (Hardman and Bell, 2017), requiring the student to correct and respond. The research concluded with these very important questions: 'How far do children benefit from the feedback they receive? Does it actually affect writing performance? Does whole-class feedback (WCF) have real value, and in what forms?' (Hardman and Bell, 2017, p. 48)

Moving from primary into Key Stage 3, teachers' written feedback continues to hold significance. For example, in secondary school English lessons, students become more familiar with their own capabilities, their developing self-regulation, the knowledge of the task in hand and the available strategies. Teaching students explicitly about 'metacognition, behaviours and emotions' (Roby, 2022, p. 13) helps fulfil learning goals, and teaching students how to self-regulate supports them in the process of engaging deeper in how and why they learn, not just what they learn. Metacognition is the awareness and understanding of one's own thought processes. Far from just thinking about thinking, it involves, developing critical thinking skills where students can plan, monitor and evaluate their own learning' (Roby,

2022, p. 75). This research focuses on written feedback given to pieces of extended writing, drawing upon a sample of four teachers and 75 students from a boys-only, independent preparatory school in England (i.e. with a high socio-economic background).

Feedback and self-regulated learning were divided into six categories:

1. planning
2. monitoring
3. reflecting
4. ambition
5. effort
6. persistence.

The research suggests that 'teacher feedback predominantly relates to the task' in hand, with 'task information used to improve future strategising' (Roby, 2022, p. 64). Observed less frequently was feedback related to the processes underlying the task, with a 'tendency for teachers to provide feedback' (Roby, 2022, p. 64) related to metacognitive approaches, rather than self-efficacy.

Put simply? The study suggests that investing time to understand students' self-regulated aptitudes can enhance feedback effectiveness. It can reduce the overall need for feedback while achieving similar or better learning outcomes.

What if we switched the focus to developing self-regulation in students instead of placing the written burden of feedback on teachers? What if we increased the uptake of peer feedback between students, teaching them how to peer-assess more methodically? In 'Increasing the uptake of peer feedback in primary school writing' (Boon, 2016), this action research reminds us that students 'learn effectively and make good progress when they are exposed to strategies, such as high-quality questioning and dialogue, written verbal feedback and self/peer assessment' (Boon, 2016, p. 213).

In the study, peer feedback was rarely used by children (aged ten and 11) to enhance the quality of their written work. Initial findings suggested that students were 'frustrated with peer assessment because their peers did not always pay attention to their written comments' and 'how the assessee might not always understand the feedback they have been given' (Boon, 2016, p. 213).

The literature review reminds us that once students have been trained to give good-quality feedback, students also need time to use and apply strategies, being held to account for how they use them. This could be achieved by asking students to document the actions that they would take next.

The study focused on children aged ten to 11, representing various levels of writing ability. The research prioritised the students' 'voice' and discovered that peer feedback increased because it was 'more useful for assessees', provided they had 'time to use it to improve the quality of work', discussing 'feedback with one another to clarify any misunderstandings' (Boon, 2016, p. 216).

It is important to add that the quality of feedback improved because student 'training involves the use of prompts and scaffolds' (Boon, 2016, p. 217), and that the paper has some excellent photographic examples from students, highlighting how their comments improved.

Moving beyond marking

I will turn now to one of my favourite EdTech platforms, Teacher Tapp, a mobile application that collects daily information from teachers every day of the year (apart from Christmas Day!). On average, they receive over 10,000 responses, providing an indicative – not representative – picture of teaching across England.

In 2022, Teacher Tapp data reported that '46 per cent of classroom teachers say that books are expected to be marked *with written comments*', concluding that although teachers are spending 'five or more hours per week marking students' work', teachers are now spending 'less than an hour marking books each week' than in previous years (Teacher Tapp, 2022). In comparison, empirical evidence and data from the Teaching and Learning International Survey (TALIS) finds that teachers are 'spending around 8 hours per week on marking' (Allen et al., 2020). As a profession, we still have some work to do.

While we should accept that written feedback has its place in the classroom, we also should acknowledge that it is one of the biggest workload burdens for teachers. The aim of this book is to provide a range of techniques and sources of evidence for teachers to use in Chapters 2 to 9 to help reduce teacher workload and give a broader source of evidence for leaders to use when evaluating student performance.

Finally, seven good principles of feedback are recommended as a model for classroom efficacy when using written feedback. How many do you currently implement?

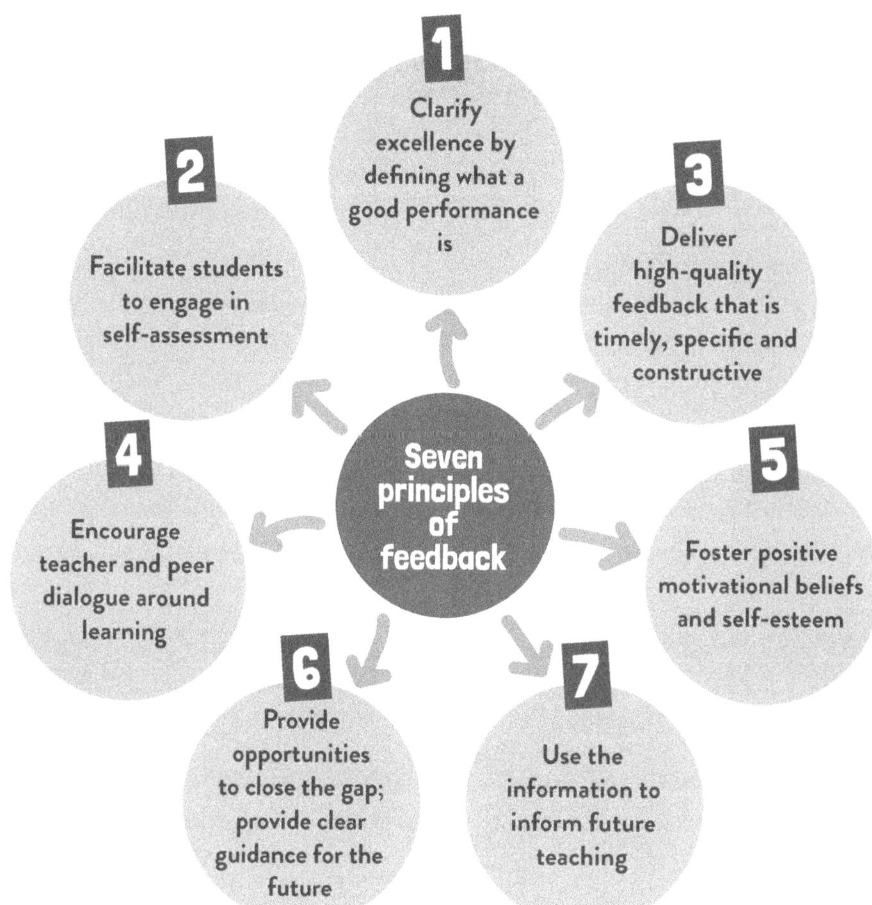

Adapted from: Nicol and MacFarlane-Dick (2006, p. 205)

We have seen that the efficacy of written feedback in promoting self-regulated learning is substantiated by research. It is not a pedagogic add-on; it's an essential component that transforms the classroom into a thriving ecosystem of self-regulated learners. The greater challenge is how we reduce this written burden on the teacher and improve responses from students.

In the next section of this chapter, we will look closely at some written feedback strategies provided by **Joseph Cash Primary School in Coventry, England**. Approximately 70 per cent of the 487 students (aged two to 11 years) speak English as an additional language, with 37 different languages currently spoken across the school. Students face significant linguistic challenges and complex social issues that impact their wellbeing. It is against this backdrop that we analyse how the school uses written feedback with Key Stage 2 (aged seven to 11 years) to help students make progress.

PRACTICAL IDEA

Case study from Joseph Cash Primary School: The Orange Box

Any quoted material in this section comes from the case study provided by headteacher Helen Nelson and deputy headteacher Sara Scott.

This practical idea focuses on leveraging the diverse and social challenges at Joseph Cash that so many inner-city schools and colleges face, shining a light on why written feedback fosters resilience for students and helps them make the required progress.

Headteacher Helen Nelson and deputy headteacher Sara Scott write: 'We believe in high-quality written feedback to help our students become passionate learners. The work of the Education Endowment Foundation, Dylan Wiliam and @TeacherToolkit inspires our teaching and learning policy.'

Joseph Cash teaching staff provide actionable written feedback, specifically the 'not yet' (*Mark. Plan. Teach. 2.0*, McGill, 2021). This is an integral part of what the school calls 'JC's Big Six', which emphasise metacognition and self-regulation. The approach is also 'mindful of staff workload in return for a high impact on the students'.

Scan to view 'JC's Big Six: Making every lesson count'

The school's professional learning is centred around working memory training (*The Teacher Toolkit Guide To Memory*, McGill, 2022) and how students learn effectively. As a result, Joseph Cash's 'written feedback is uncomplicated, not a list of symbols, codes, multicoloured pens or lengthy comments'.

Scan to view JC's 5 Weekly Must Haves

Therefore, according to 'JC's 5 Weekly Must Haves', the school's use of written feedback is minimal and 'Orange Box marking' (see below) is a key element of the school's policy. This practical approach ensures that staff focus on their students' linguistic challenges and provides students with a clear focus, effectively moving learning forward in smaller chunks.

To improve student outcomes, the 'Orange Box' method is a written chronological feedback strategy.

1. It identifies a key area for improvement.
2. This key area for improvement is further enhanced by live assessment in the lesson
3. Other elements of the policy include P+ and P-, which are linked to students' presentation, e.g. has it improved or declined?
4. All teachers mark with an orange pen; this is a **deliberate** decision, choosing a less intense colour than red, but which still stands out.
5. Students then edit their work in purple pen. This allows teachers to see that students have responded to their written feedback and improved their work.
6. Students record the 'focus' for each lesson, and they receive either a tick or a 'not yet' to support the learning sequence and engage them with their learning process. This also helps students identify key knowledge.

Success for Joseph Cash in implementing the 'Orange Box' method has been achieved through a deliberate focus on language, purpose and impact, without detrimentally impacting teacher workload. Nelson and Scott write that 'buy-in across the school has been achieved through consistent instructional coaching sessions and listening to feedback from staff'.

Scan to take a look at one example of the Orange Box method

The impact this approach has had on students at Joseph Cash is that they are more successful and confident in lessons and participation in class has also increased.

1. Use the Orange Box approach to offer students manageable feedback.
2. Teach students how to access support.
3. Design peer-assessment opportunities to develop ownership.
4. Build students' resilience by providing time for them to redraft their work with access to teacher advice, which helps the editing process feel more manageable and familiarises them with constructive criticism.

WORKED EXAMPLE

Using the 'Orange Box' method and the 'not yet' technique, students never feel like they have failed; they are simply **not** there **yet**! At Joseph Cash, the student voice shows that students understand and like how teachers support them to make progress.

Here is how to use the technique.

1. Take a look at this example from the school:

Scan to view an example of a teacher using the Orange Box method to feedback

2. This is a vocabulary exercise in Key Stage 2 science, in which you use the 'Orange Box' method to highlight a specific area where the student's work needs improvement.
3. This approach reduces your workload and focuses the student's attention on a narrow and manageable area to improve. Helen Nelson says the 'impact of this can be seen in students' written outcomes and how they feed back to peers. Students feel proud of what they achieve and the progress they make.'

4. Next, and where relevant, use the 'not yet' technique. See a written example of the technique below, to indicate where the student has not yet met the criteria:

Scan to view an example of the 'not yet' technique

5. ABC – Agree, Build, Challenge; use questions to encourage deeper thinking.
6. In this reading example, the student responds to the feedback in purple pen:

Scan to view an example of a student responding to feedback

7. 'Assessment journals' are used by Joseph Cash teachers to capture whole-class curriculum themes, next steps and individual actions.
8. Joseph Cash says that 'During instructional coaching sessions, always reflect on this question: Are pupils making progress as a result of your feedback? This ensures we constantly identify ways to improve student outcomes, reduce workload and work [in an] even smarter [way].'

At the heart of successfully implementing the ideas posed by Joseph Cash, the approach requires an understanding that specific written feedback approaches must meet the needs of primary school students, especially for teachers working in a challenging context, used to enhance both the academic and pastoral curriculum.

TEMPLATE

Using the Orange Box

Joseph Cash's approach can be used in all subjects and with students of all ages. It can also work in one-to-one scenarios, small groups or whole classes. Helen Nelson and Sara Scott write that 'written feedback can have a huge impact on students' development, but it also needs to be concise, purposeful, and manageable for teachers to keep moving learning on'. How you use formative evaluations will largely depend on the age of your students and the subject in hand. The choice of colour helps reduce teacher workload and helps students to focus in on one area to improve.

Here is a blank template to help you implement the same approach.

Scan to download a copy of the template

1. Identify a key area to improve (Teacher marks specific improvement with an X)			
Knowledge	Skill	Literacy/numeracy	Presentation

2. Provide detailed, actionable feedback (focusing on the selected area for improvement)
Text entered here by the teacher/expand this area
Not yet *(Rather than frame the work as incorrect, use 'not yet' to indicate the area in which the student hasn't met the criteria)*
'Not yet' comments: • Text entered here by the teacher • Text entered here by the teacher

3. ABC: Agree, Build, Challenge feedback (To encourage self-regulation and a dialogue with the student's work, pose targeted questions or statement)
1. Agree: What went well? 2. Build: Suggest one area to improve. 3. Challenge: Pose a question to challenge thinking.

4. Student action plan (Encourage the student to reflect and plan their next steps)
Changes needed:
Strategies to use:
Questions I have for the teacher:
Follow-up notes:

CHAPTER 2

WRITTEN FEED-UP

Written feed-up is defined as written communication that aligns student efforts with their learning goals and clarifies expectations. (Feed-up = Where am I going?)

In the **written feed-up** approach, a student submits their work and you provide a grade but, specifically, you **compare** how far the student is from their target grade. This method focuses on goal-setting and helping students to understand their progress in relation to their objectives. But what does this look like in practice? How do you avoid students looking at the grade and either giving up or not acting on what they should do next? This introduces an interesting challenge for all teachers.

A degree of self-regulation by the student is required in order to act (feed-up) on the assessment you provide. Students need to have a degree of knowledge already available to them to be able to act on your assessment. In order to do this effectively, students will need to be taught metacognition (see Chapter 1) so that they can develop **critical thinking skills**.

Critical thinking is the ability to plan, monitor and evaluate one's learning. All of this helps us to understand how this influences the nine types of formative assessment I identify throughout the book.

Dollis Primary School, the case study school in this chapter, offers a practical perspective on how their teachers use **feed-up** effectively, including the way this strategy can motivate students by making their learning goals and progress transparent.

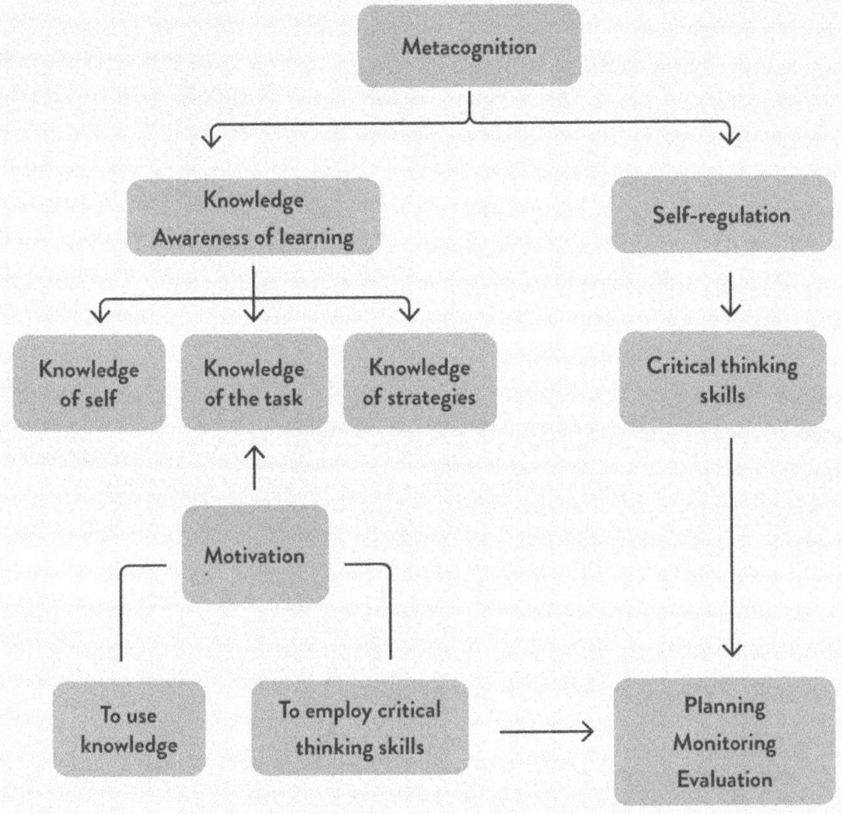

Adapted from *How to Create Autonomous Learners* (Moir, 2023)

I will also explain how you can use *this type* of formative assessment in an encouraging and constructive way, rather than a subconsciously discouraging way that could impact students' self-esteem. This may be so easily done when students are provided with a written (or spoken) grade and, as a result, students may switch off from future feedback.

EXPLAINER

If you search Google Scholar for 'feedback, classroom feed-up', you will only find approximately 2,000 search results. Searching 'feed-up' alone returns 14,000 entries (April, 2024). Research suggests that, academically, this phrase is relatively new, despite publications about the concept dating as far back as the 1800s!

Let's consider some of the historical research and publications about feed-up.

In the publication 'The Jewish educational system–a plea for organic unity' (Dushkin, 1932), the phrase 'feed-up' appears in one of its first academic papers. The short paper aims to promote unity and cooperation among teachers and leaders, in order to uphold the educational system's integrity, challenging the notion that one system is more important or better than another. The phrase 'feed-up' is used to imply that it is better to 'strengthen existing school systems that are organically alive, than to create them anew' (Dushkin, 1932, p. 79) – that it is we who should provide the system with the resources it needs to grow.

More recently, in 'Feed-up, feedback and feed-forward: Re-examining effective teacher–student interaction', Anderson (2012) presents an exploration of feedback research, highlighting the significance of teacher–student interaction for developing student motivation, satisfaction and learning. The study sought to understand students' perceptions and influences on their learning, through classroom observations to understand teachers' perceptions and practices regarding feedback. Findings reveal varied levels of understanding about feedback and awareness of feedback methods, most of which focused on task completion, with a need for more comprehensive understanding that includes feed-up and feed-forward. I have to be honest: after 25 years in the classroom, I only came across these terms in 2020, so they're still quite a revelation to me, and from what I see on my school and college visits, it's also the same for many of you!

Are you looking at how you can bridge the gap between teaching and learning? How to offer a fair and rigorous school and college policy for your colleagues and students? How you can balance the burden of traditional marking with what you know about good formative assessment?

My intention in this chapter of the book is to demonstrate some evidence to help you and your school or college move beyond a traditional understanding of 'marking' and 'feedback'.

Teachers who participated in Anderson's research showed a basic understanding of feedback, and much of the focus rested upon students accomplishing 'a given task (feedback) and not why they were engaged in the task (feed-up) or what a potential next task might be (feed-forward)' (Anderson, 2012, p. 190). The research highlights the need for teachers to enhance their understanding of feedback too.

In a final example, 'The representation of feedback literature in classroom observation frameworks' (Ruelmann et al., 2022) offers an excellent literature review on feedback, feed-up and feed-forward. 'One criterion (feed-up) was not captured by any (lesson observation) framework' used in the study (Ruelmann et al., 2022, p. 67).

The research theory reminds us of the importance of assessment as a critical driver for 'enhancing student learning, and an important aspect of teaching quality' (Ruelmann et al., 2022, p. 69). Rather than viewing 'feedback' as information delivered, we should consider **how formative assessment is used**.

In the context of 'feed-up', the paper defines this as the gap between the 'current state of learning and the target state' (Ruelmann et al., 2022, p. 71). In summary? Much of what happens in any lesson observation between you and the student happens away from observer eyes. The paper further defines 'feed-up' as 'learning goals: ensuring the success criteria are clear (encouraging students to "look up" and to ask where am I going?)' (Ruelmann et al., 2022, p. 71), and recommends that you should ensure gaps in learning are well-defined, specific and challenging. Goal-related formative assessment that is clearly linked to success criteria, including new, challenging goals, is how you could differentiate between providing **feed-up**, feedback and feed-forward.

Training teachers to explore how different types of feedback, particularly feed-up and feed-forward, have evolved and how they can be used today is important and will help to inform future practice.

In the next section of this chapter, you will meet **Dollis Primary School in Barnet, London**, a two-form-entry school with 424 pupils (aged two to 11 years). It is highly diverse, particularly linguistically, with 88 per cent of students speaking English as an additional language (EAL), significantly higher than the national average for EAL students. What makes the school very interesting is that a significant proportion of children do not live locally.

PRACTICAL IDEA

Case study from Dollis Primary School: Tackling the tricky bits

Any quoted material in this section comes from a case study provided by headteacher Rosetta Dyer.

The focus of this practical idea is Dollis Primary School, a case study of Key Stage 1 students (aged five to seven years). You will see how **written feed-up** is showcased and how teachers provide a grade to **compare** how far the student is from their target grade. You will discover how the school evidences a range of positive outcomes from some of the students' exercise books.

When I asked headteacher Rosetta Dyer why written feed-up was a particular strength at her school, she said: 'Written feed-up is an embedded approach within our marking and feedback policy. Across the curriculum, this strategy is adapted to ensure written feed-up is accessible and purposeful for the students. For example, in Key Stage 1, written feed-up can be represented pictorially to allow the children to edit their work and meet the targets set.'

Scan to view an example of written feed-up

The school achieves this by involving staff in policy design to gather their input and suggestions. This means all staff 'have a secure understanding of the policy'. Rosetta continues, 'In all students' books, we have produced a student-friendly reference sheet to ensure students understand the meaning behind the assessment provided. This is adapted for different subjects and individual needs to ensure that all groups of students receive high-quality written feed-up.'

As in most schools and colleges, subject and school leaders review student exercise books and provide teachers with developmental feedback. Students' voices are gathered so that their views are incorporated into future teaching practices; the pupils understand the **feed-up** so that they can use the formative assessment to make progress.

When I asked the headteacher to provide evidence of how this method improves student outcomes, she said that all students receive **written feed-up** to ensure they have opportunities to progress over time. Data collection suggests that students take pride in their work and enjoy reading their assessments. Building in the time for this technique ensures that students are keen to respond, providing the students with the opportunity to take greater independence over their learning. As a result, students become aware of their achievements and the next steps to take.

TOOLKIT TIPS

1. Provide students with assessment-friendly stickers or sheets inside their exercise books.
2. Provide written feed-up, proportionate to curriculum time, to encourage active engagement with the success criteria.
3. Use visual tools, such as a timeline or assessment thermometer, on classroom walls to offer students a visual checklist to help them see, and monitor, their progress.

WORKED EXAMPLE

Scan the QR code below to see some examples of what written feed-up looks like in practice at Dollis Primary School.

Scan to view an example of 'Tackling the tricky bits'

For example, in mathematics, students use an embedded approach called 'Tackling the tricky bits', where an anonymised piece of work from the day before is used to challenge misconceptions.

In English, Rosetta explains that 'students are given time before any new material is taught [and] space to edit and embed written feedback, to further improve their writing and subject knowledge'. Teachers may prompt students to look at spelling errors or letter formation, helping students to independently seek the tools they need to edit. For example, scan the QR code below to see this in Dollis's phonics working wall.

Scan to view an example of embedding written feedback

So, what could this look like for you in practice?

1. Here's how you could provide your students with a marking and feedback crib sheet to be fixed to the front of their books:

Scan to view an example of the Dollis marking scheme

2. These assessment criteria outline how you have communicated written feed-up to the student.

3. Give students an opportunity to explore and understand how to embed any knowledge or skills, or how to edit their work further.
4. Provide students with a non-negotiable checklist or a 'must, should, could' chart.

Scan to see an example of a non-negotiable checklist

These suggestions are additional successful approaches to help students align their learning goals with the assessment expectations.

When I asked Rosetta how other teachers, schools and colleges could apply Dollis Primary School's ideas into their context, she said, 'The adaptations we have made to our policy have been particularly effective. Adding symbols, teachers ensure that all students embed **written feed-up** before any new learning is taught.'

If you want to try using these techniques, I would recommend building additional time into your lessons. Rosetta recommends 'an additional five minutes' at Key Stage 1 to factor in time for students to respond to teacher **written feed-up** assessment.

TEMPLATE

Using 'Tackling the tricky bits' as an example

In this chapter example, I showed you how you can add value to students at such an early stage of their school life. Written feed-up indicates work completed, signposted with a current assessment, compared against future potential.

Here is a blank template to help you implement the same approach.

Name:	
Date:	
Title of work:	
What is the misconception?	
Current assessment?	Grade 9 8 7 6 5 4 3 2 1
Target assessment?	Grade 9 8 7 6 5 4 3 2 1
Assessment criteria:	
Immediate action required?	
Self or peer assessment	
What will you do?	
You must: **You should:** **You could:**	

Scan to download a copy

CHAPTER 3

WRITTEN FEED-FORWARD

Written feed-forward is defined as written advice on future tasks, guiding students on how to apply their learning in upcoming scenarios. (Feed-forward = Where to next?)

Written feed-forward is the **final** aspect of the feedback, feed-up and feed-forward trilogy – another crucial aspect of formative assessment in the classroom. In this approach, you will focus on **providing guidance** for the student in written form, **explaining** what they can do next to improve their work or learning process.

The 'guidance' in this form of assessment type is important. Research indicates that feed-forward enhances learning when it 'supplements current learning' achievements (feedback) (Zarrinabadi and Rezazadeh, 2023) but also provides additional guidance on attaining future learning objectives (looking ahead: how can I advance?) (Hattie and Timperley, 2007; Nicol and Macfarlane-Dick, 2006).

A forward-looking assessment method is particularly useful as it helps students to understand how they can apply what they've learned to future tasks, as well as with the immediate task in hand. You already do this implicitly, every day and in every lesson. My goal for writing this book is to help you become aware of all the nine approaches outlined in the Introduction on page xi, and select and use each strategy explicitly when working with students.

With feed-forward, the premise in this chapter is that you **explain in written form** how a student can improve their work. The amount of detail given will, of course, depend on whether the student is three or 18 years old, i.e. on the age and understanding of the the feedback recipient.

It could be the case that the phrase 'feed-forward' is new to you. As a teacher, I am confident that you will already be providing explanations, particularly in written format.

In this chapter, we will discuss how teachers can effectively communicate suggestions for future improvements in written format. This will, for example, include specific written strategies teachers can use to encourage students to progress towards larger objectives.

Waverley School, for students aged four to 19 years, is the case study school in this chapter. The case study will explain how **feed-forward** is adapted in a range of subjects.

EXPLAINER

A model for effective feedback, first hypothesised by Hattie and Timperley in 'The power of feedback' (2007), argued that feedback can have different perspectives:

1. 'feedback' (comparison of the actual status with a previous status
2. 'feed-up' (comparison of the actual status with a target status
3. 'feed-forward' (explanation of the target status based on the actual status).

Additionally, all forms of feedback should reduce any deficits and 'may be reduced through a number of different cognitive processes, including restructuring understandings, confirming to students that they are correct or incorrect, indicating that more information is available or needed' (Hattie and Timperley, 2007, p. 82).

Several years later, in a new meta-analysis of empirical research, Wisniewski et al. argued that 'feedback cannot be understood as a single consistent form of treatment' (2020). Clearly, only using the phrase 'feedback' is heavily **outdated**, especially across education.

Therefore, in this chapter, as per the 'The representation of feedback literature in classroom observation frameworks', feed-forward *literature* is defined as supporting the 'assessment of current learning (feedback) with further [explained] information on **how to achieve** learning goals (looking forward: How do I make progress?)' (Ruelmann et al., 2022, p. 72).

Exploring different subjects

On Google Scholar, it is possible to search for three subjects and how these relate to feed-forward in the context of a secondary school:

1. a core subject
2. an English Baccalaureate (EBacc) subject
3. a non-EBacc subject.

We can focus on 'written' and 'feed-forward' (as search terms) in the context of a secondary classroom, and the resulting academic research can provide us with some examples of how you can help students make progress in written form.

1. Written feed-forward in a core subject (English)

Does feedback facilitate student learning? In 'Students' experiences and responses to feedback in a Finnish EFL [English as a foreign language] classroom', Pollari (2017) asks 'to feedback or to feed-forward?' For context, it's worth considering how English is taught as a foreign language, especially in this context. For students who lack substantial knowledge, feedback, in all its forms, is more crucial than ever. This study showcases how Finnish students acted on feedback in an English context where students might not have prior knowledge, striving to provide 'more Feed [Forward] **during** the learning process and not only after it', offering more balance and personalised learning (Pollari, 2017, p. 29). Feedback considers the journey, whereas feed-forward factors this in, but also considers the future progress needed and the methods required to make that progress too.

As a reminder, providing more feedback doesn't mean that you are providing better feedback. Knowing how a student responds to teacher feedback benefits progress.

In this same study, students studied English for almost ten years, totalling between 700 and 800 lessons. Students studied 'six compulsory and two advanced courses of Advanced English' (Pollari, 2017, p. 16), and 'although feedback seems to guide and facilitate our students' learning quite adequately... teachers should pay more attention to feedback [in EFL] teaching'(p. 20). Two main research questions were asked (which relate to the Pollari research):

1. What are students' experiences of feedback?
    a. Do they feel they get enough feedback?
    b. Does the feedback facilitate and guide future learning?
2. What kinds of responses to feedback did the students have?

With regard to feed-forward commentary in the research, from 199 students, '146 answered the questionnaire'; 65 stated that they 'wanted feedback that was personalised (18 mentions), actionable and tangible (15), ongoing and timely (5) as well as constructive and balanced (5)' (Pollari, 2017, p. 17). Interestingly, 16 students hoped for 'personal oral feedback from the teacher'; note that this is in **addition** to written feedback!

2. Written feed-forward in an English Baccalaureate subject (history)

In another study, students working as peer assessors without teacher intervention 'were able to fairly accurately infer levels of quality for most of the work' (Wimshurst and Manning, 2012, p. 458). The research examined formative assessment (feed-forward) as an intervention, requiring students to evaluate previous students' exemplar work (rather than traditional feedback in which the teacher marks the students' work).

Key findings suggest a significant improvement in the quality of students' summative assessments after participating in the feed-forward exercise. So, which recommended approaches should teachers therefore use when implementing written feed-forward? How you deliver written feed-forward will, of course, differ for a four-year-old compared to a 16-year-old.

3. Written feed-forward in a non-EBacc subject (art)

Finally, my third example of feed-forward looks at how it can be applied in a creative subject. The research undertaken for this, 'Using student goal setting and feedback to encourage independent learning' (Carmody, 2019), discusses enhancing the drawing skills of Australian secondary school students in Years 7 and 8. In a study spanning 18 months, teachers focused on building students' confidence using a range of interventions, including effective feedback. The paper reflects on why 'feedback should always be accompanied with the inclusion of learning goals'; without any link to assessment, it will **not** always be effective.

Throughout the study, artwork examples from students are provided, along with a narration of how feedback is offered using distributed practice (spacing the learning over time) and explicit instruction (teaching in a direct and structured way), where students who achieved well 'were the ones who consistently completed the reflection'.

So, as we reach the end of our third chapter and the three main types of assessment and research around them, you should now have a better understanding of why we need to move on from the phraseology of feedback and marking. **'Why only feedback?'** This is a question we should all ask one another when we hear any discussions about formative assessment.

There are many pitfalls for providing just feedback:

1. It is often given in written form without explanation.
2. It focuses mainly on the task, and is often not seen again.
3. It is often combined with a grade.
4. It focuses mainly on weaknesses rather than strengths.
5. Students only have one opportunity to receive feedback and improve. (adapted from Lindner, 2017, p. 6)

Research conducted with female students aged 15 to 22 years (n = 210) suggests feedback significantly improved student self-regulation, while 'presenting feed-up and feed-forward, whether together or in isolation, significantly improved' student motivation (Zarrinabadi and Rezazadeh, 2020, p. 588).

In the next section of this chapter, you will meet **Waverley School**, which is part of **Waverley Education Foundation, located in Birmingham**. Waverley has state-of-the-art facilities, catering for children aged four to 19 years, with 600 students in the primary phase and 1,150 in the secondary and sixth form phase. The work of the students and staff is underpinned by their common principle, **'learning through diversity'**.

PRACTICAL IDEA

Case study from Waverley School: The KFC approach

Any quoted material in this section comes from the case study provided by school leaders across the trust: Satnam Dosanjh, Darren Gallagher, Umar Malik and Hailee McAuley.

Waverley School has a unified vision for assessment. Central to their approach is a shift that has redirected their attention from just enhancing an individual piece of work to the holistic development of the student.

With a focus on Key Stage 2 in this chapter, Waverley students are empowered to showcase newfound knowledge in a range of contexts and subject scenarios during subsequent lessons. School leaders across the trust, Satnam Dosanjh, Darren Gallagher, Umar Malik and Hailee McAuley, say they have achieved this by using the DfE's Marking Policy Review Group report 'Reducing teacher workload' (2016), insights from the Education Endowment Foundation (EEF)'s 'Teacher feedback to improve pupil learning' (2021) and, I quote: 'the wisdom shared in Ross's book *Mark. Plan. Teach.* (McGill, 2017) and resources from the @TeacherToolkit website'. Their 'primary teaching and learning model has been influenced [by these], particularly for assessment'.

Scan to take a look at a primary teaching and learning guide

The school leaders say that 'after discussions as a senior leadership team about the vision and direction, staff training was dedicated to a comprehensive whole-school discussion on teaching and learning, introducing this new shared approach called: Assess–Plan–Teach'. A deeper and more dedicated reflection towards understanding assessment has helped Waverley shape their one-page teaching and learning approach.

Their policy work serves as a go-to reference for primary staff, contributing to the development of a streamlined feedback approach that improves clarity but also alleviates staff workload.

So, the key question is: How has this method improved student outcomes, and what do the formative assessment method ideas look like in practice?

Waverely's strategic and rounded approach to formative assessment celebrates all aspects of classroom feedback, particularly actionable **written feed-forward**. Their students not only grasp the need for improvement, but they also gain opportunities to apply learned skills. For example, when mastering a technique to 'calculate ten per cent', this becomes a tool for future reasoning of other percentage calculations. Or perhaps there may be **written feed-forward** comments given by the teacher for a student's narrative on suspense writing, which include the repetition of words (for example, 'something', 'somewhere', etc.); the future outcome translates into improved overall storytelling.

Scan for an example of written feed-forward for suspense building in writing

Scan for an example of written feed-forward building character traits in writing

School leader Umar Malik says that the 'practical application of this assessment approach empowers students, equipping them with critical thinking skills they can gradually self-regulate'. This has a ripple effect across Waverley that extends beyond academic achievements, improving behaviour and student attendance.

Here are five tips I would recommend you consider when reflecting on the research on written feed-forward, and Waverley School as a case study.

TOOLKIT TIPS

1. Always provide students with clear objectives and success criteria.
2. Use 'next steps' comments rather than just 'right' or 'wrong' task-specific commentary. Remember, feed-forward requires an explanation. Given that this chapter highlights working with younger students, the details provided will need to be relevant to the student receiving any guidance.
3. Use visual aids to show complex concepts, to explain how future tasks can be completed. Diagrams, maps and objects broken down into chunks and clearly signposted against all assessment criteria will add significant value.
4. Teach students how to assess their own work, using feed-forward diagnostic thinking. For example, rather than 'This is a good piece of work, Ross. You should explain what you mean about XYZ to improve your work', instead, your written feed-forward should say, 'Ross, to improve your understanding of ABC, you should incorporate one example of DEF and elaborate on VWX to explain how ABC works.'

Scan to see an example of feeding forward

5. Keep comments positive, specific and focused. Always benchmark the next step up in the assessment process to help **feed the process forward!**

In the next section of the book, I have provided you with a worked example scenario to show you how to bring this technique to life.

WORKED EXAMPLE

So, what does this look like in practice? In English lessons, Waverley teachers have used **written feed-forward as an explicit technique** to improve writing skills. During 'shared reading' lessons, Waverley students analyse texts to recognise and understand, for example, 'the purpose, audience, structure, and language'. These features are then systematically taught throughout dedicated (future) writing sessions, where students are 'tasked with crafting their adventure stories into varied contexts'. **Written feed-forward** as an explicit strategy can be used to emphasise the application of learned skills in future scenarios. Another example includes a character description task, providing evidence to show how written feed-forward helped students grasp the effectiveness of employing the *'the more, the more...* sentence' technique to describe character traits in greater detail.

In mathematics, students often face the challenge of multiplying fractions. Waverley provides students with **written feed-forward**, offering 'a rule like the "KFC approach" (Keep, Flip, Change) to assist in solving calculations' (see below). This technique, successfully applied to future scenarios, aligns with the school's 'focus on memory and some fundamental principles emphasised by Ross during a visit to our school to deliver *The Teacher Toolkit Guide To Memory* training. He highlighted the importance of building a bank of concepts, facts and rules to enhance knowledge recall from long-term memory.' This important perspective has contributed to Waverley's effective use of feed-forward as an assessment approach.

Here's a simple teacher-to-student scenario to model the process:

Teacher: Mr McGill introduces the concept of 'decorative techniques' found in a range of fabrics in a Year 6 textiles lesson. He reminds the students to use the 'KFC approach' (Keep, Flip, Change) when improving their design ideas for making a T-shirt.

Student: Ross uses the 'KFC approach' on his A3 sheet of paper while reviewing his draft drawings for a T-shirt. He has a range of pencil sketches displaying a 4x4 car printed on the shirt. He continues adding pencil colours and describing his technique to make the 4x4 car stand out as a 3D layer on the shirt, for example by using sequins or glitter.

Teacher: Mr McGill observes Ross's work and notices that Ross wants his T-shirt to be made from sequins, which does not meet the assessment criteria requirement of having a pattern or a 3D print on the T-shirt fabric. The teacher writes on Ross's work in the feed-forward section of the paper: 'Explain how your third design idea is 3D.'

Student: Ross reads the teacher's comments and refers to the assessment criteria. (The student has a little 'A-ha moment' to themselves, which the teacher observes at a distance.)

Teacher: As the teacher walks away and stops to record comments in other students' books, the teacher reminds the class by questioning some pupils for a good definition of 3D objects found in the classroom.

Student: Ross now edits his annotations, making clear changes to his final drawing. His cotton T-shirt will be coral green in colour, with a gold-sequined silhouette of a 4x4 car centred on the chest. Whether Ross can make this pattern, and whether he can label and spell 'silhouette' on his drawing is a question to revisit on another day...

Teacher: The success of this strategy is that the teacher has used an in-class (live) formative assessment opportunity to help feed the learning forward. Noticing the error, then asking for a written explanation of the misconception, is a low-stakes route to improving self-regulation.

Scan for examples of the KFC approach being used on a problem-solving maths task with two different students

In conclusion, whether you teach three- or 14-year-olds, how could other teachers, schools and colleges apply this to their classroom? Waverley places 'assess' at the beginning of their teaching and learning process to 'enable informed future planning of the curriculum'. This ensures students act on feed-forward to make progress. This approach guides future curriculum planning and in-class decision-making, and fosters students' critical thinking skills.

TEMPLATE

'Keep, Flip, Change' template

In this section, I have provided a blank template for you to use in future professional development discussions or in the classroom with your students.

Written feed-forward	
Student name	
Date	
Topic (knowledge)	
Misconception?	
Action required	(The teacher circles various codes to speed up the process.)
Student action	The teacher writes one thing the student must do next. (Codes are explained below to help students.)

Scan to download a copy of the template

CHAPTER 4
VERBAL FEEDBACK

Verbal feedback is defined as immediate, spoken responses to student work or actions, providing direct and interactive communication. (Feedback = How am I going?)

Verbal feedback offers immediacy and can be extremely engaging for the student. It's also a perfect approach to help you manage classroom motivation and the dreaded burden of written commentary. All teachers tell me they provide verbal feedback, but they struggle to articulate their methodology when I ask them to describe their verbal feedback technique.

Having structured conversations with students provides the opportunity to discuss how a student's piece of work can be improved. When the conversation is considered alongside carefully crafted questions to engage students in a dialogue (see *The Teacher Toolkit Guide to Questioning*, McGill, 2023), you can provide students with opportunities for immediate clarification and deeper understanding. It is important to have a structured methodology that you can automate time and time again.

Given that we have already defined what feedback is, it's worth noting that 'feedback' can be verbal as well as written. One key question that emerges is how do we evidence verbal feedback for quality assurance processes? Parents, inspectors and school and college leaders should be comfortable that the verbal methods used are robust and that the evidence gathered is varied, substantial and often unseen by observers. So, how is any evidence achieved?

To help answer these questions, I have completed some research in this area by conducting a case study of seven schools across England. Commissioned by UCL, Associate Professor Mark Quinn and I set about working with 13 secondary state school teachers from seven disadvantaged state schools, across the subject range (McGill and Quinn, 2019).

Included in the sample were teachers who were working in schools with a high proportion of disadvantaged students. These were typically settings in which teachers were required to 'mark once a week' (Teacher Tapp, 2019) in the traditional sense (written feedback).

The project's objectives were to improve student outcomes and offer a solution to the increasing issues with teacher workload and mental health. Quinn and I wanted to evidence methods of live assessment to demonstrate whether there would be a detrimental or positive impact on student outcomes if teachers completely removed or significantly reduced written feedback. Throughout this and the following two chapters, I will answer this question by drawing out some verbal assessment recommendations that aim to alleviate the burden of written feedback, and aligning them to the principles of feed-up and feed-forward.

EXPLAINER

You know that verbal feedback works. It's immediate, efficient and adds huge value when motivating students. If delivered well, it can be transformational for your workload and wellbeing, and for student outcomes. However, as a profession, teachers struggle when asked to evidence anything that is not written down in students' books. The existence and efficacy of verbal feedback may seem unclear to people who conduct quality assurance processes in our schools and colleges. I'll remind you of that important message again: feedback is for one purpose only – the students.

Almost a decade ago, I became increasingly frustrated with the pressure placed upon teachers and school and college leaders to provide 'evidence'. I became impatient with the lack of understanding observers showed when visiting various students or subjects, and how limiting their evidence base could be. Evidencing live assessment in class for observers who are not present at that moment makes teachers' life much harder for them! Observers' rebuttal to any claims about progress is often 'Show me the evidence', which adds unnecessary workload for others. This may be simply because observers cannot do the hard thinking for themselves. Or they do not have a range of sources at their fingertips that can provide concrete evidence of, for example, the way in which you deliver verbal feedback and how this feedback can be inextricably linked to student outcomes, other than summative grades.

Another possible problem is that school and college leaders and teachers do not have enough confidence to demonstrate how verbal feedback with students in class can be evidenced by other sources, and not written commentary and grade progression. The perception that 'marking is king' (written feedback) and that it is a reflection of your hard work should be questioned and ultimately rejected.

Taking these lived experiences and frustrations into account, I pitched a research project to UCL, which was approved for the academic year in 2018/19, as mentioned in the Introduction. This research, titled 'UCL Verbal Feedback Project report', (McGill and Quinn, 2019), was conducted with seven disadvantaged schools and aimed to assess the impact of verbal feedback on student engagement, particularly among disadvantaged students in Years 7 and 8. The project also evaluated the effects of this (verbal) feedback method on teachers. Thirteen teachers collected evidence of changes in their practice and in student outcomes, maintaining reflective journals to document their findings.

The case study trial concluded that verbal feedback, when implemented effectively, positively impacts student engagement and teacher wellbeing, and appears to have no detrimental impact on students' outcomes (McGill and Quinn, 2019). The research highlighted the importance of professional development in enabling you, as teachers, to transition from traditional written feedback towards verbal methods, which are timely for students, and give weekends back to teachers – **no more marking books on a Sunday night, all alone at your kitchen table!**

Scan here

At the time, this research contributed significantly to the understanding of other feedback methods in classrooms. It challenged traditional practices while offering a viable alternative that benefits both students and teachers. Today, classroom teachers are more familiar with live assessment methods, but I suspect some teachers still struggle with the evidence base for verbal and non-verbal feedback outcomes. How can they 'prove' that such assessment is working effectively?

Evidence is available that shows how teachers' verbal feedback to students who are difficult to teach can add value, especially when it is a 'positive, praise-based strategy for encouraging all pupils' work' (Swinson and Knight, 2007, p. 253). On the other hand, there may be instances where verbal or non-verbal feedback is not effective, which represents another reason for finding a way to monitor and evidence the effectiveness of this feedback, so any areas for improvement can be identified. For example, Swinson and Knight found that teachers tended to provide students with 'a high proportion of negative feedback directed towards their social behaviour and almost never praised them individually about their appropriate behaviour' (2007, p. 253). This is hard to keep track of on a case-by-case basis, but becomes evident if there is a record over time.

It's also worth asking, 'How do students themselves perceive verbal feedback?' This needs serious consideration to ensure our technique has the required impact. In a study involving a rural mixed secondary school in Cornwall, research focused on four Year 9 students over 11 weeks. This study – 'Exploring student perceptions of verbal feedback' (Kerr, 2017) – revealed that students view verbal feedback as a distinct form of communication, characterised by focused conversation centred on personal and task goals. 'Students identified "signal points" which turned [their] conversation into verbal feedback... where cues are significant pieces of information relating to how to progress.' (Kerr, 2017) These 'cues' are what will be significant in the latter chapters of this book – verbal and non-verbal gestures (cues) will shed light on how teachers and schools can develop a wider range of formative assessment methods to support teaching and learning, particularly teacher workload and student outcomes, in the broadest sense. For example, 'cue recognition' is the ability to identify and interpret specific signals.

Visual and auditory cues are essential for helping individuals respond to their environment. For example, a student could observe what the teacher is saying through their facial gestures and body language, to deepen their understanding of the feedback being given.

This is why I first proposed the Verbal Feedback Project to UCL (McGill and Quinn, 2019) and, five years later, why I wanted to document how my thinking and evidence base have evolved since. Gestures and non-verbal and verbal commentary in classrooms add significant value.

In one final research recommendation, an early academic contribution to the verbal feedback discourse, 'The nature and value of teacher verbal feedback' (Zahorik, 1967, p. 1), asks 'What types of verbal feedback do teachers use and how frequently do they use them?' An astonishing **175 types of feedback were used** by teachers, with **16 types** being used frequently! 'The study consisted of obtaining and analysing transcripts of tape-recorded lessons to provide data concerning feedback use and relationships, and obtaining student perceptions of teacher, verbal feedback to provide data relative to feedback value.' (Zahorik, 1967, p. 3) The research suggested that the types of feedback teachers use were dependent on a range of factors. Still, the one with the greatest value was 'the value of the pupil response' (Zahorik, 1967, p. 5).

In the next section of this chapter, we will examine three verbal techniques: verbal feedback, verbal feed-up and verbal feed forward, and how these manifest themselves in our classrooms. In this chapter, we learn how **Delta Independent School in Consett, County Durham, uses verbal feedback strategies**.

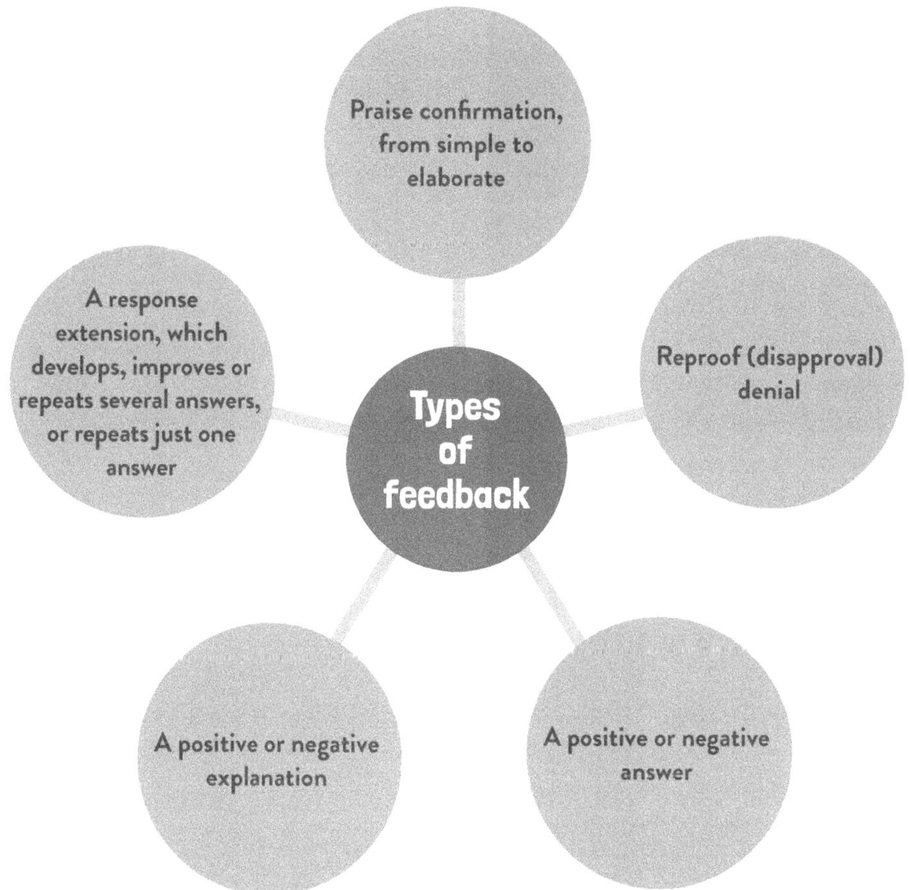

Adapted from Zahorik, 1967

PRACTICAL IDEA

Case study from Delta Independent School: Positive praise strategy (PPIPL)

Any quoted material in this section comes from a case study provided by deputy headteacher Ryan Curran.

In this section, you will learn how teachers provide verbal feedback strategies in a range of subjects and, more specifically, how they provide evidence for quality assurance outside students' exercise books.

Delta Independent School is an alternative provision located in County Durham. The school offers provision for 13- to 16-year-old students who have not succeeded in mainstream education for one reason or another, providing students with wrap-around care to meet their needs. This is provided as a bespoke programme set out by the mental health lead, or a comprehensive and tailored special educational needs and disabilities (SEND) plan set out by the SEND coordinator (SENDCo). The school currently has 46 students on roll, 21 of whom have SEND, and 96 per cent of the students receive free school meals.

I asked deputy headteacher Ryan Curran why verbal feedback is a particular strength at his school. He replied, 'Delta encourages teachers to deliver verbal feedback to our students, tackling misconceptions in the lesson. It is also used widely in our wrap-around support to provide immediate advice and guidance to our students.'

Delta ensures that all students' needs are met. Interestingly, it started life as an outdoor centre, providing outdoor education and activities for local disadvantaged young people, offering this service to schools and colleges before demand from the local area asked for more academic provision. The nature of the school, its students and how the teachers are encouraged to work helped it to become the fully registered school it is today.

I asked Ryan how he achieved that and he explained how their 'staff team has undergone hours of training on developing strong relationships with our students'. This has enabled their teachers to learn how to communicate with their students much more effectively. As a team, they meet every Wednesday evening for CPD and have explored what verbal feedback looks like in the classroom.

Scan to hear directly from Ryan

Part of their success rests with their mental health and behaviour team, who have spent many hours with each student, getting to know their backgrounds and experiences. Throughout their training sessions, students are provided with verbal feedback, such as on how they have improved their listening, motivation to change or engagement in the lesson. 'This motivates students to learn more about how to develop new learning strategies to improve their anger, self-esteem, depression, body-image, self-harm or anxiety,' Ryan tells me. These important training sessions then feed into the teachers' planning, exploring any concerns or positive feedback to help support and boost the confidence of that student.

I then wanted to know how their verbal feedback methods improve student outcomes. Ryan said, 'Verbal feedback has improved student engagement within lessons; students have become more confident as their understanding of topics improves.'

Scan to see evidence of how their practical techniques influence student outcomes

Due to the efforts of Delta teachers, using immediate verbal feedback to highlight misconceptions and to support and challenge student behaviour or understanding must significantly impact students' learning in the context of alternative provision. Teachers must sharpen their skills to work with students who are more vulnerable and cognitively require further support.

Drawing upon past visits to the school, here are some key recommendations from the research and practical examples they use.

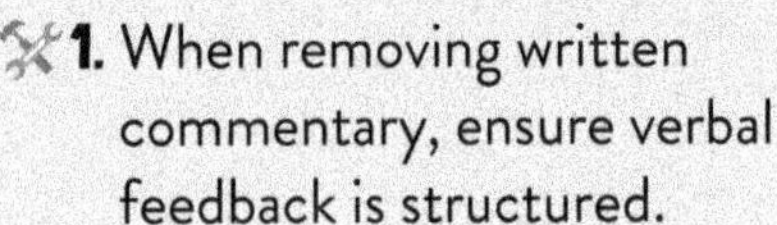

1. When removing written commentary, ensure verbal feedback is structured.
2. Be clear and precise. Ensure feedback is concise and actionable.
3. Verbal feedback should provide a reference to the work to date, motivating students on the effort and completion.
4. Develop 'positive praise strategy' scripts (explained in the next section), to ensure feedback motivates rather than demotivates the learner to do more work!
5. Finally, think about student outcomes in the broadest sense: attendance, punctuality, engagement in lessons, 'hands up' in class, classwork completion, uptake in subject admissions, student mental health, sanctions and rewards. There are so many ways schools and colleges can evidence how verbal feedback improves other aspects of school and college life.

In the next section, you will see a walk-through example of some of these ideas in practice.

WORKED EXAMPLE

Praise, probe, identify, plan and lock (PPIPL)

Guided by Delta's teaching and learning policy (scan the QR code on page 42 to view), verbal feedback has played a substantial role in improving the attendance of some of their students. These students feel more confident and supported when in school. Before I share my practical idea, I asked Ryan to **provide some examples of what this looks like in practice at Delta Independent School.**

He replied that 'Feedback is personalised, not just a token "well done" comment. We have identified that there are a number of students within our school who are not the most resilient. Therefore, we have removed phrases such as "wrong answer", replacing them with "not yet". This takes away the negative elements of these words and encourages students to push themselves to find the correct answer.'

Since introducing this, the school has found that students are engaging more in their lessons, resulting in better outcomes.

Scan to see the school's data in science

Student welfare is also improving, year on year; scan to see the evidence from 2022/23 and 2023/24

Here is a step-by-step explanation of what a **'positive verbal feedback script'** might look like in the classroom. I want you to imagine a 14-year-old student in an English GCSE classroom at the start of the academic year.

Teacher: *(As they walk around the room, the teacher approaches Amjad's desk.)* 'I see you have chosen the image of the town library for your story, Amjad. What a fascinating building! What is the key idea you are exploring in your assignment?'

Student: 'I am trying to write about a ghost story that happens in the library. My grandfather told me about the ghost, and the people he says have seen it.'

Teacher: 'A ghost story? Gosh! Don't forget that your first paragraph must hook in the reader. I notice yours is very dramatic, describing the atmosphere of the library and the facade of the building. That's a really strong start. Well done!'

Student: 'Aw, thanks, Miss. I thought it was too boring.'

Teacher: 'No, not at all! It's very engaging and your use of nouns and verbs really hooks the reader. I'd love to read your next attempt in, say, ten minutes?'

Student: 'Sure, Miss. What about if I describe some of the people who work inside the library?'

Teacher: 'Nice idea. Oh, and don't forget, every author who writes a book edits their first attempt, several times. Have you looked in the school library for any ghost stories?'

Student: 'No, Miss. Great idea! I'll go at lunch.'

And there you have it. A verbal feedback conversation that adds a significant amount of intrinsic motivation and a story told at home that captured the imagination of the student. Teachers achieve this every day in classrooms across the country. Now, how do we evidence that little bit of magic captured by hundreds of thousands of teachers up and down the country?

Verbal feedback has a significant impact on reducing the workload of teachers. Schools and colleges that not only facilitate verbal feedback in their teaching and learning policies but also empower teachers to see, hear and practise how to use these techniques explicitly are happier places to work.

Ryan Curran, deputy headteacher, stated: 'We have given teachers the autonomy to work with their students in the way they see appropriate. When our teachers provide verbal feedback, they ensure that:

1. both they themselves and the student are listening actively, accommodating the feedback conversation
2. they consciously use body language to signal attention
3. they work sensitively to build confidence and clarity
4. they understand the goal of verbal feedback as a formative strategy
5. they support students to act immediately and show them how to take action
6. they make conversations explicit and encourage students to interpret feedback collaboratively
7. they use open questions to raise awareness, reveal beliefs and enable the student to act.'

Verbal feedback has to be meaningful; it also must enable the student to take action. I then asked Ryan how other teachers, schools and colleges could apply this to their context.

He replied that 'verbal feedback goes beyond simply telling a student what to do. For it to be purposeful, students must know what to do next, independently. Therefore, investing as much time in developing metacognitive strategies for students is equally important to developing formative assessment methods for teachers to use with their students.' Delta Independent School exemplifies how it is always worth remembering that, as well as knowing your students well, your school staff must also know what language to use and what to avoid.

Before I share a blank verbal feedback template with you to try, let me offer ideas for quality assurance and evidence sources to demonstrate how verbal feedback impacts a range of student outcomes. Of course, how verbal feedback is used, with whom, how, why and how often will all be influencing factors, but for now, consider that you are using a brilliant methodology for delivering verbal feedback, which leads to an improved level of intrinsic motivation in your students. Imagine the following:

1. **Attendance records:** These can show that absent students now turn up because they feel valued, and receive regular dialogue about how well they are doing, rather than perhaps waiting several days or weeks for written comments that they 'couldn't be bothered to read'.
2. **Punctuality records:** Students are never late but they love your lesson! Imagine if your school/college had punctuality issues, but in your lesson, as a result of your verbal feedback scripts, students know you love and challenge them? That shift in punctuality data would be demonstrable evidence.
3. **Enrolment:** Students choose your subject for GCSE options or for their A level courses.
4. **Questioning:** Students always want to respond, because they know you will never shut them down with rebuttals. You evidence this in lesson observations or SEND students feeling able to respond to difficult concepts.
5. **Rewards and sanctions:** Students are receiving more rewards and fewer sanctions, compared to periods when you and your colleagues were focused on detailed written commentary. The result? Teachers are free to feed back verbally, having more time to plan lessons, share rewards and praise comments with students and families and, as a result, the data suggests sanctions are reducing!
6. **Extra-curricular:** Uptake in after-school/college activities have increased because students want to spend more time with the teachers they believe value their efforts. They don't want to go home!
7. **Student-led initiatives:** The student community starts to show they love where they are taught, leading events and volunteering in the local community. They are happy to offer their free social hours to designing drama concert stage sets or spending endless hours preparing for the school/college exhibition or open evening.
8. **Teacher reflections:** When teachers speak about their students, reports reflect positive sentiment analysis (commentary). There are fewer public criticisms of students in public spaces such as the staffroom. Appraisal documents and an uptake in exit interviews show how much teachers share positive comments about the student community. Perhaps teacher retention gets better too?! Imagine that...

9. **Behaviour and engagement:** Student behaviour improves across the school/college because students start to see and feel that their teachers care. This is no different to any other school, but as a result of reducing the written burden and improving teachers' opportunities to work immediately, students feel valued, with clear actions provided so that they can improve their work and their overall grades.

10. **Completion rates:** Finally, fewer students are excluded, they complete all their courses and examination results slowly start to improve – all because teachers use more efficient methods for engaging students with their work, and school and college leaders improve their perspective. They no longer need evidence that teachers must provide written commentary for isolated work scrutiny and observations in the future, but instead, opt for a broader data collection in their quality assurance processes to determine that if the teacher is providing purposeful feedback – in whatever form – student outcomes will improve across the board.

Try using my blank template on the next page to improve how you structure verbal feedback. This next technique is my number one go-to strategy!

Scan for a 'Scripting, structured feedback' resource

TEMPLATE

Stages	Your prompt	Notes during conversation
Praise (Step 1)	**Refer** to any known previous actions to validate previous effort. For example, how far has the student moved forward in the available time? List specific strengths and what impact their actions have had.	
Probe (Step 2)	**Ask** some probing questions, then narrow the focus. For example, 'Why did you do it this way?' Note the responses.	
Identify (Step 3)	**State** the issue and make clear two or three actions, plus any required support. It is preferable to ask the student to generate the possible options. Hold back your opinions if you can.	
Plan (Step 4)	**Plan** ahead and set a timeline. What are the barriers/risks? What support is needed? Make an explicit note of dates and timings.	
Lock (Step 5)	**Lock it in**: Make sure the student knows exactly what to do next. How committed are they? Ask them to summarise the conversation and state clearly their next steps. Make a note of their commitments.	

PPIPL feedback script

This is a feedback script I have used for over a decade, which is now being used by school mentors who support early career teachers as part of the Early Career Framework (ECF, DfE, 2019). It works brilliantly for classroom feedback conversations, and also in other scenarios, such as working with the teacher for lesson feedback. It can also be used with students in 30-second conversations in the corridor, for managing low-level behaviour or when 'sitting beside' students when discussing a piece of work. it would be important to adjust the timeframe for different scenarios. For example, short feedback conversations could be completed in 30 seconds, whereas for lesson feedback, the script could be used during a 15-minute conversation after school.

Scan to download a copy of the template

In another scenario, I've used this technique many times for managing difficult conversations with colleagues, or in phone calls with parents and families. One word of caution: in the last stage, do not ask a parent to repeat back the conversation in summary, as it might appear condescending! However, in a lesson feedback conversation, you might want the teacher to confirm what has been discussed so you can check for understanding to see whether next steps are clearly identified.

CHAPTER 5

VERBAL FEED-UP

Verbal feed-up is defined as oral clarification of learning objectives, helping students understand and focus on their targets.
(Feed-up = Where am I going?)

Verbal feed-up is the practice of verbally communicating learning objectives, goals or targets to students. It is a formative assessment strategy that focuses on helping students understand what they are aiming for in their learning, comparing their actual performance to their target grade. So, for example, I may be a student participating in a group role play for a drama GCSE performance and in the rehearsal, the teacher pulls me to one side and asks a powerful question: 'Have you considered what would happen if you did X or Y at this point in the performance?' The choice immediately poses a couple of options for me. By delivering the question with a powerful and prolonged pause, the teacher ensures their face gestures remain neutral (see non-verbal gestures in the Introduction on page xx). This means that they do not offer any further ideas, thus empowering me to do the thinking for myself. This simple and effective technique is timely, and ensures that I can re-engineer my performance before the final exam.

In this context, the definition of 'verbal' refers to the use of spoken words, not written or non-verbal gestures. This approach considers the use of tone, pace and choice of language used by the teacher, which we will explore later in this chapter with our case study school, Everton Free School in Liverpool.

The use of verbal communication is direct and interactive, allowing for immediate engagement and clarification. How this is balanced with providing target status assessment will require context-specific translation to suit the situation.

When you speak with students, how do you currently discuss targets and grades? Do you have a specific methodology that you repeat time and time again? What would be the benefits of automating your verbal feed-up to make your working life a little easier? How do you distinguish between verbal feedback and verbal feed-forward?

In the latter part of this chapter, I will look at how you can clarify or set targets for your students. This involves communicating what success looks like and what the students are working towards, aligning students' efforts with their objectives and assessment criteria, as well as helping them to understand the purpose and direction of their learning activities and possible goals. Our case study school will provide a useful example to consider in your practice, and we will evaluate how this technique can be used to motivate and guide students, providing them with a clear understanding of what they need to achieve and why it is important.

EXPLAINER

It proved more of a challenge to locate academic research on verbal feed-up (where am I going?) strategies than other assessment strategies.

In the context of teacher education, I managed to locate 'Where to next? Examining feedback received by teacher education students' (Ellis and Loughland, 2017), which reported that 'there was little evidence that supervisors referred to the overall goals... Feedback pertaining to "Where am I going?" was rare... [Feed-up was] **not** always provided with a clear purpose, goal or objective' (p. 55). It was assumed by the supervisor and the trainee teacher that supervisor feedback would be offered to develop the trainee's practice!

At this point, let's analyse whether any of us can name two or three specific feed-up strategies that we use in the classroom.

What I have learned from researching and writing this book is that feed-up (where am I going?) and feed-forward (where to next?) are implicit things that we do as teachers, but being able to explicitly reference a strategy that aligns with what these types of feedback are remains a challenge for many of us.

I would now like to share research-based strategies that are intended to provide you and your colleagues with the professional insight to help drive your teaching and learning forward. In Ellis and Loughland's research, in the context of teacher supervisors who provide feedback to trainee teachers, they conclude that 'feedback was far more prevalent than both feed-up and feed-forward' (Ellis and Loughland, 2017, p. 59).

At the time of writing, we clearly have much work to do if we have experienced teachers who are unable to distinguish feedback types when working in a range of scenarios, especially when training the next generation of teachers.

In a study carried out by Eriksson, Swedish primary school teachers and students shared concerns regarding classroom feedback provided to seven- to nine-year-olds. What is enough but not too much? Just right is, however, not easy to narrow down, as it is relational and dependent on how the individual student interprets the feedback (Eriksson, 2021). The research revealed that there needed to be a mutual understanding and a degree of trust.

The students' ability to interpret and adapt feedback was also paramount, with the need for personalisation. Again, digging into the details, I found there was a paucity of any classroom-based research in which explicit references are made to feed-up strategies, or those with any correlation to student outcomes.

The study concluded that a main concern 'was to construct clarity in what the other communicated' regarding trustworthiness and understanding of feedback (Eriksson, 2021, p. 22). Knowing that feedback can be trusted is central to it being an effective intervention in classrooms. It also underpins the importance of relationship dynamics in the feedback process and highlights the need for you to adapt your feedback strategies to individual student needs and perceptions. The diagram below expands on this.

Perspectives and concerns in student–teacher classroom feedback interaction

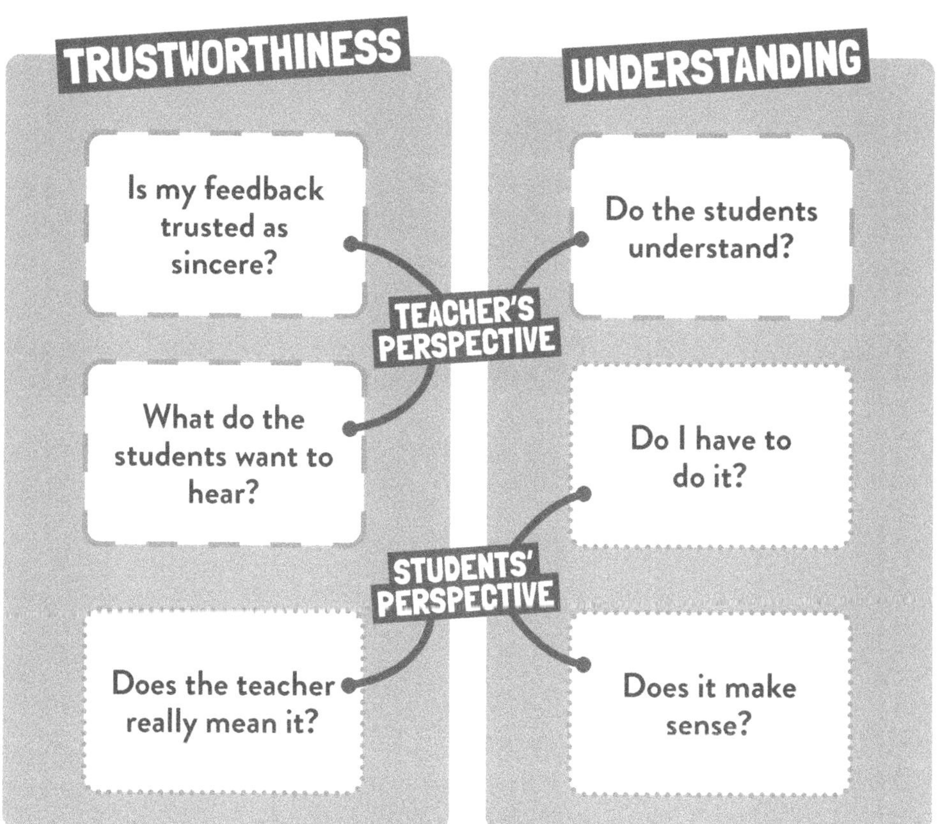

Adapted from Eriksson, 2021

In 'Revisiting "The Power of Feedback" from the perspective of the learner', Mandouit and Hattie (2023) offer insights into student perceptions and feedback types, including the effect on learning, motivation and emotion, as well as the variables. For example, what type of feedback is actioned? (See the Introduction, page xxi: feedback, feed-up, feed-forward and the figure showing Hattie and Temperley's model of feedback (2007).)

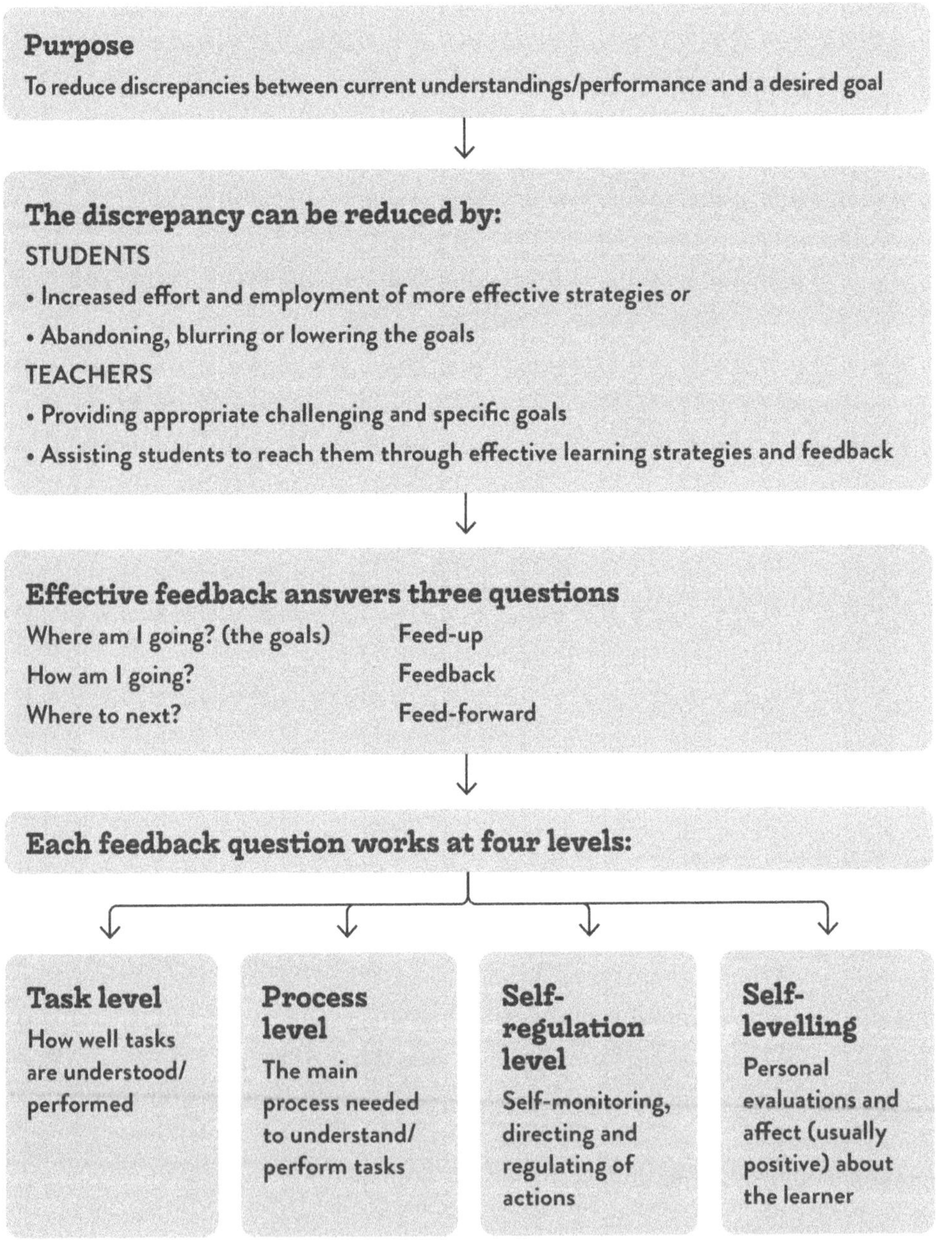

Purpose

To reduce discrepancies between current understandings/performance and a desired goal

↓

The discrepancy can be reduced by:

STUDENTS

- Increased effort and employment of more effective strategies or
- Abandoning, blurring or lowering the goals

TEACHERS

- Providing appropriate challenging and specific goals
- Assisting students to reach them through effective learning strategies and feedback

↓

Effective feedback answers three questions

Where am I going? (the goals)	Feed-up
How am I going?	Feedback
Where to next?	Feed-forward

↓

Each feedback question works at four levels:

Task level
How well tasks are understood/performed

Process level
The main process needed to understand/perform tasks

Self-regulation level
Self-monitoring, directing and regulating of actions

Self-levelling
Personal evaluations and affect (usually positive) about the learner

In an excellent contribution to the 'feed-up' discourse, it can be helpful for you to learn how to categorise feedback types. Feed-up strategies can include a mixture of your prompts to support students, as well as explicit strategies to use in the classroom. For example, feed-up prompts can include:

1. sharing the learning objectives
2. showing what success can look like
3. assessment criteria
4. 'what a good one looks like' (WAGOLL).

In 'A matrix of feedback for learning', Brooks et al. (2019) offer a range of novice, professional and advanced suggestions to help teachers differentiate between feed-up, feedback and feed-forward. There are 'excellent practical examples of formative assessment, underpinned by evidence' (p. 26) to help your students to self-regulate their learning. This feedback matrix can support you to understand what you currently do, and where you can develop any missed opportunities in the classroom.

Scan to download a copy of this fantastic feedback matrix!

Other suggestions include teachers sharing key ideas, planning key questions and sharing the skills and strategies students need to use to be successful.

Classroom strategies to support feed-up include a mixture of:

1. refining slideshow slides or other teaching materials to reduce cognitive load
2. providing worked examples
3. helping students to identify misconceptions
4. allowing students to diagnose misconceptions by self-assessment
5. existing tools such as knowledge organisers and checklists to help students establish their progress towards objectives.

PRACTICAL IDEA

Case study from Everton Free School: Prompting up

Any quoted material in this section comes from a case study provided by English teacher Tim Waldron.

In this chapter, our case study features **Everton Free School, an alternative provision setting in Liverpool** with 120 Key Stage 3 and 4 students on roll (aged 11 to 16 years). The school serves students from all over the city, Merseyside and the Wirral, many of whom are from deprived areas. We will use the study to explore how **verbal feed-up** strategies are used, and how this technique is quality-assured without any written evidence (commonly sourced in students' books).

I asked English teacher Tim Waldron why feed-up was a particular strength at Everton Free School. He replied, 'Students have struggled in mainstream, and we seek to build their confidence. Verbal feed-up affirms to students their ability to meet their goals, from lesson objectives to personal targets.'

The school achieves success using a variety of feed-up methods. In particular, teachers question students' understanding of vocabulary in the lesson. Waldron stated that 'we may challenge what students understand or what the lesson objective means'. Teachers adapt their teaching to rephrase formative assessment to help students understand and engage with their classwork. Teaching assistants also play an important part in clarifying these objectives and targets with students.

You may ask students how well they understand something using a 1–10 scale. This is essentially what verbal feed-up looks like. Similar to a traffic light system, this self-assessment by number methodology can be spoken with confidence (or not), depending on the student and also how they feel about their own performance.

Scan to see an example of a feed-up slideshow

You can confirm or clarify something to help students engage with the objectives. This often involves simpler language or more relevant examples to help students understand what they should be doing.

Tim continues: 'One-to-one **verbal feed-up** with students is key to how we help students reach their targets and understand objectives.' Completed by teachers and teaching assistants, this informal mentoring approach helps them clarify and affirm students' understanding of goal setting, i.e. 'Where am I going?'

Talking **with** students is a significant part of the formative assessment process. SEND students (for example, those with autistic spectrum disorder, or ASD) benefit from the one-to-one feed-up, 'which helps them receive clarification, then take action more readily'.

I then asked Tim how these techniques add value to each student and to the school's overall performance, i.e. how verbal feed-up improves students' outcomes, and what this looks like in practice.

He replied that 'This process gives students ownership of their targets. It also provides space for teachers to clarify what is **not** being said, reducing any misconceptions of what is and is not expected of them.'

In an alternative provision setting, many students do not need additional barriers put in front of them. Effective verbal communication helps students make progress, so building confidence first is likely to result in further progress. Offering affirmation and encouragement to complete objectives and targets means that a great deal of praise is offered. 'I know you can do it' comments encourage students to push on, says Tim.

At Everton Free School, expectations are challenging and realistic. Tim comments: 'We have high expectations, but sometimes we make their targets achievable; we build confidence first.' The reality is that self-confidence often inhibits them.

Teachers using explicit **verbal feed-up** methods have improved student outcomes from A to B, and this can be documented outside of students' exercise books.

Scan to see the front of the school's exercise book

Scan to see inside the school's exercise book

TOOLKIT TIPS

1. Clearly articulate the learning objectives to students.
2. Provide live demonstrations: model how to be successful.
3. Engage students individually, providing specific actions for improvement.
4. Prompt students to reflect on what they should do next.
5. Facilitate small-group discussions, providing past work as examples.

In the next section of this chapter, we will explore a worked example of what this looks like in the classroom.

WORKED EXAMPLE

Here are some examples provided by Everton Free School of a teacher using verbal feed-up in the classroom.

Scenario one: Student A would arrive at the lesson and sit at the back of the class because of severe social anxiety. They wouldn't want to stay in the lesson. Over nine months, with the help of a teaching assistant using a mentoring approach, Student A moved from the back of the class to the front. They soon regularly attended school and eventually sat their GCSE examinations. The verbal feed-up approach was used in the lesson, in the first instance for attending class frequently. The teaching assistant helped to relay the information personally, with lots of affirmation. Verbal feed-up was used to help clarify and support the student with their class attendance and understanding of the lesson subject.

Scenario two: One of the school's many success stories includes a previous student returning to work as a teaching assistant. Student B was misunderstood in mainstream education and moved on from secondary school to alternative provision. They were associated with a gang outside of the school. This student was taken under the care of one of our maths teachers. The teacher used verbal feed-up for discussing targets, especially aspirational target-setting, to help Student B realise their potential. This small shift greatly influenced Student B and eventually saw them pass their exams and begin an apprenticeship with a community support service. The student has gone on to complete their Level 3 teaching assistant certificate and has eventually come back to our school to work as a teaching assistant. We now believe not only that our processes have supported this student, but also that their experiences will enrich the lives of many others in our school community to come.

These two examples provide evidence of what you can do as a teacher.

Implementing verbal feed-up explicitly as a strategy needs time to embed. Teachers and support staff must be able to clarify and affirm students' understanding. For example, rephrasing and simplifying vocabulary (not changing the meaning) doesn't mean negating academic language but helping students to understand it. Tim Waldron says the process 'engages students with learning and gives them confidence'. As a top recommendation, I would suggest giving students some time to receive feedback after delivering any lesson objectives.

Sitting beside the students to talk through their targets is a powerful and immediate intervention all teachers can use. Providing space in your classroom is an important part of this, as is the methodology. However, putting aside this additional time is a luxury in other settings. Verbal feed-up does lead to positive change, and you can evidence this technique in student outcomes and the quality assurance processes you use.

Returning to an earlier comment, how do you evidence verbal feed-up? Other than looking in students' exercise books, quality assurance methods that you could use, for example, include mapping before-and-after attendance data, completion of work, participation in lessons (shown by reward points), student surveys and satisfaction scores.

TEMPLATE

Verbal feed-up prompting template

This template provides you with a step-by-step series of prompts to follow:

Stage	Teacher prompts:
1. Objective	Share lesson objectives
2. Initial assessment (e.g. a planned question)	
3. Strategies (For the teacher to use)	Show what a good one looks like (easy) Share success criteria (easy) Use graphical representations (medium) Increase task complexity (medium) Reduce exemplar material (hard) Use coaching prompts (hard)
4. Verbal feed-up (Response from teacher)	(Write down) 'Today I am…' (easy) 'What you need to do is…' (medium) 'How are you using the success criteria?' (hard)
5. Student response/actions:	
6. Agreed actions:	

Scan to download a copy of this template

CHAPTER 6

VERBAL FEED-FORWARD

Verbal feed-forward is defined as spoken guidance on future improvements, advising students on next steps for better learning outcomes. (Feed-forward = Where to next?)

Verbal feed-forward is focused on future tasks and improvements to work, requiring a verbal explanation from you, as the teacher. You will guide students by providing clear, actionable steps about what to do next in order to enhance their learning or performance.

Verbal feed-forward can be particularly useful in encouraging students to think critically about how they can apply their learning in new contexts. This is why metacognitive strategies such as self-explanation ('in your own words') or elaboration ('tell me why') need to be taught to students in classrooms and throughout the curriculum. It is not something that should be left to chance, nor is it something that should be taught to students for only a few months in revision assemblies just before they sit their final exams. You should involve students regularly to help them develop an awareness and regulation of their learning process, which is **central to their ability to use feed-forward** effectively.

In this chapter, we will delve into how teachers can offer **verbal feed-forward** guidance that is actionable and relevant to each student's needs. When teachers provide verbal feed-forward, they are not just giving information on what to do next, they're also encouraging students to think about how they learn, plan and apply these strategies. This is how we can start to teach students to think metacognitively.

It is highly likely that you already explain verbally to your students what they should do next. My challenge to you is to consider how you could automate this process. How could you pass this strategy onto somebody else? If you think carefully about how you structure your verbal conversations that help students move forward, how could we design a strategy that you could use in 30 seconds or in five-minute conversations?

Later, I will introduce you to Kennet School in Berkshire to explain how they practise feed-forward across the whole school. The teachers demonstrate how these verbal techniques are applied in order to provide valuable insights into ways of adapting verbal feedback strategies to meet student needs, especially neurodiverse students. We will also explore how you can frame feed-forward assessment to foster metacognitive skills, in order to guide students to set their own specific goals, reflect on their own learning strategies and evaluate their own progress.

EXPLAINER

Feed-forward (where to next?) is something that every teacher provides in every single lesson: it is spoken guidance to students on future improvements. These 'what next steps to take' guide the student on their future path. This is something I would like you to consider when widening your professional understanding of marking and feedback. Something else worth considering is: What is your explicit technique when explaining (feed-forward) to a student what they should do next? Do you have a specific methodology to make your work life a little easier?

In Duncan's small-scale action research project, '"Feed-forward": Improving students' use of tutors' comments' (2007), students were asked to use 'old feedback comments against new tasks' (p. 278) – that is, effectively feeding forward. When providing students with any form of assessment, the research suggested that the key question to ask is: What do students do next with the comments from teachers? All the research I have read in this area continues to return to this critical question.

Students said that 'the absence of identified areas for improvement meant that analysing the... comments [from their tutors] in order to construct feed-forward was very difficult' (Duncan, 2007, p. 278). The research concludes that how and why teachers provide feedback can be improved to raise students' learning. For example, 'Improving students' learning by developing their understanding of assessment criteria and processes' was a two-year research project by Rust, Price and O'Donovan that focused on tacit and explicit knowledge transfer to help develop students' understanding of assessment criteria (2010).

The intervention used criterion referencing – using test scores and statements to describe performance – evolving from the late 1990s to help to develop consistency between examination moderators. As a result, a common criteria assessment grid was developed and 'first piloted in the academic year, 1997–98. The grid provided 35 criteria plotted in matrix format against grades resulting in "grade definitions"...' (Rust et al., 2010, p. 149). The hope was that the grid could offer students 'explicit guidance (resulting in better work), and making it easier to give effective feedback to [them]' (p. 149).

The intervention design provided a 90-minute workshop to students, followed by student discussions in small groups, discussing their initial individual assessments. The small groups then agreed the grades, followed by a tutor-led comparison of example work for each criterion.

Student groups then reviewed their assessments in light of the tutor's explanation, with a final report from small groups for each piece of work. The tutor then provided annotated and marked versions of samples and discussed the assessment.

Overall, the results suggest that this simple intervention, taking **a small amount of time**, could have longer-term and transferable effects!

The grid experiment suggested that staff and students wanted a 'discussion to support the use of the grid' (Rust et al., 2010, p. 151). What is very difficult to determine is what verbal feed-forward techniques are best used in this approach. While this is an interesting piece of research, we don't know what methodologies were promoted in the verbal discussions.

When we change the search phrase 'verbal' to 'oral', there is a much wider evidence space available. In one paper by Koen, Bitzer and Beets, 'Feedback or feed-forward? A case study in one higher education classroom' (2012), the phrase 'oral' is used for speech feedback, and the phrase 'non-verbal' is used in the context of gestures and body language (see Chapters 7 to 9).

Koen et al.'s research makes an important point: when teachers provide oral feedback, it 'motivates students to engage in the learning process' (p. 235). When students receive oral feedback, they can engage in a conversation and ask further questions for clarification. The biggest change for teachers is the workload associated with trying to ensure commentary is provided to all students, as and when required. The challenge for teachers is: how do you evidence that these things have taken place in a way that reflects the value of conversations?

When teachers have conversations with their students, these moments are a valuable learning tool to help communicate any issues, and to suggest possible routes forward for the students. 'Very few would argue about the importance of offering students the opportunity for seeking clarification.' (Koen et al., 2012, p. 236)

Some of the difficulties for teachers are how to provide 'oral feedback in a forward-looking way that prompts thought and reasoning while also promoting student engagement' (Koen et al., 2012). We know the frequency of feedback matters, as does the value of self-assessment to promote learning.

Learned peer assessment can help students understand criteria when applying this with their peers. 'Feedback on understanding of the task may have to be linked with feedback on the learner's understanding of the criteria used.' (Black and Wiliam, 2006, p. 28)

In Coe's article, 'Can feedback improve teaching?', specificity and the structure of feedback are also important, 'determined by the type of "performance" which it is desired to influence' (Coe, 2006, p. 46). Whether we consider feedback, feed-up or feed-forward, it is not the details that improve learning, but rather the way students understand the feedback and how to use it. This leads into metacognition territory once again. **Teaching students how to learn must also therefore include how to learn from feedback throughout the learning process.**

Feed-forward equips students to monitor their learning and to become reflective, self-directed learners. Therefore, students and teachers alike must also learn the differences between feedback and feed-forward!

It is important for us all to remember that we should not assume that all students will understand our feedback, no matter how brilliant, accurate and detailed it is. Always ask yourself: How will my students use this information?

For many years, prior to the COVID-19 pandemic, I was already experimenting with online tools to facilitate sharing video commentary with my audience. This was used for a mixture of teacher training sessions, as well as general responses to questions that flood in via the @TeacherToolkit website. What I learned very quickly is that engagement improved significantly as a result of video or audio commentary, rather than just by text. Today, I use this information prior to visiting any school I work with. I share a very short pre-CPD teaser to prime training material.

The analytics are very insightful, reminding me of the importance of keeping content to 70 seconds or less(!) and allowing me to determine which teachers are engaging with the content, for how long and at what particular points. Although engagement improves, this is a good reminder of the technological world in which we now live. This experience adds to growing evidence of how our working memory *struggles* to focus and reminds me of how important verbal commentary is in the classroom.

In 'Moving feedback forward: Theory to practice', Orsmond et al. (2011) 'provided opportunities for students to "rate videos" and leave verbal comments' (p. 243). This encouraged dialogue between the students and teachers, increasing engagement and providing comments for future work (feed-forward).

Orsmond et al. (2011) show which new models of feedback were delivered compared with the usual approaches used. Some examples of new feedback delivery include encouraging dialogue between the giver and receiver of feedback or involving peers, and feedback on the assignment process. Some examples of standard feedback delivery include monologues that are tutor-directed and do not involve peers, and feedback on assignment product.

Self-regulation features once more, with dialogue and a practical framework used to guide practice. The GOALS framework is used:

- G = Goals oriented and linked to criteria
- O = Observable aspects of students' work
- A = Actions required
- L = Learning opportunities
- S = Strategies going forward.

This research highlights the crucial role of feedback in learning, and how traditional feedback methods can be inconsistent, resulting in apathy and low student satisfaction.

I suspect most teachers feel like this, i.e. that the teachers provide more detailed and useful feedback than students perceive. It's worth exploring whether this is true in your classroom. 'Feedback [must] be part of a dialogic process' (Orsmond et al., 2011, p. 242): it must involve discussions with students so that they recognise their strengths and weaknesses.

Plus, as students are generally so immersed in technology – at home, in particular, and in school, when opportunities are provided – the use of audio and video feedback can provide richer, more engaging feedback for them.

In summary, feedback is a transformation practice, but teachers must work explicitly to encourage students to actively engage with and apply feedback to their learning.

In the next section, we will explore how **verbal feed-forward** strategies add significant value to student progress, without anything being documented on paper! We learn how **Kennet School in Thatcham, West Berkshire**, has implemented inclusive feed-forward ideas into their curriculum and pedagogy.

PRACTICAL IDEA

Case study from Kennet School: Chasing misconceptions

Any quoted material in this section comes from a case study provided by assistant headteacher Sam Martin.

Kennet School is a comprehensive academy in Thatcham, West Berkshire, with 1,800 pupils aged 11 to 18 years. The school has two specialist on-site provisions: the physically disabled resource (PDR) and hearing resource base (HRB), expertly equipped to support various needs within a mainstream setting. Kennet prides itself on being research-informed and innovative in its practice.

Verbal feed-forward is a particular strength at the school because pedagogy has been carefully crafted and refined post-pandemic. Techniques used are framed by the school's Seven Principles for Learning. This shared language of evidence-based practice provides a framework and toolkit to ensure consistency for both staff and students.

Scan to view the Seven Principles for Learning framework

One of the principles named is 'feed-forward'. This encompasses the processes involved in low-stakes and formal assessment and, most crucially, 'checking for understanding' before directing students to their next steps for improvement. This area is a particular strength at the school, as it draws together many other principles, such as creating a purposeful climate for learning as teachers move around the classroom, actively monitoring students at work and supporting adaptive teaching pedagogy.

Sam Martin, assistant headteacher at the school, says, 'Verbal feed-forward has become synonymous with particular strategies we use: the practice of live assessment in class, which is explicit in every classroom, studio and playing field.' The strategy involves teachers moving around the classroom to 'live-assess' students' work by reading what they have written, watching how they work or listening to what they say. As a result, the teachers can respond immediately to capture the steps required to help move students' work forward.

They have achieved much success at the school due to the evolution of 'live marking' in each classroom. This, they say, is 'supported by our commitment to whole-school training on teaching and learning, anchored to several pedagogical foci. Examples include checking for understanding, providing targeted feed-forward information and creating a purposeful learning environment.'

Framing these strategies as multi-purpose has strengthened staff investment in them (for both experienced and less-experienced teachers), reducing their workload and helping students to take action.

Sam says, 'In addition to whole-school training, there have been more regular micro-training sessions in "Principles for Learning" briefings. These seven-minute mini-training sessions provide an ideal platform to share best practice, reiterate the non-negotiables and provide support on where the strategy provides flexibility.' This approach keeps the profile of verbal feed-forward high on the agenda, and ensures 'staff continue to experiment'.

Scan to view an example of a training document shared in a staff briefing

Strategies have been paired with quality assurance processes to produce alternative sources of evidence that go beyond students' exercise books. This whole-school focus and support has meant 'the culture inside each classroom has shifted significantly over the past 12 months to one that is proactive, purposeful and engaged', with an understanding of the stage each student has reached and how to feed-forward.

Kennet School also puts a 'Feed Forward Week' in the calendar! This provides a point in time for staff and students to reflect on 'where to next?': the future path of assessment and possible outcomes. Feed-forward takes many guises, but a particular strength at the school is the use of verbal whole-class feed-forward, tackling common misconceptions through precise reteaching, remodelling or retesting. In these dedicated lessons, students are directed to act upon this feed-forward advice and to rectify or redraft immediately to eliminate errors. In this case, the evidence can be seen in lesson observations and during informal learning walks. The evidence is clear that these methods are part of teaching and learning culture at Kennet.

To help move the dialogue away from solely resting with traditional marking or lesson observation, how does this method improve student outcomes and what evidence can Kennet School provide? In response to verbal whole-class feed-forward, students' engagement and resilience to reflect have improved. This is mirrored in the outcomes of the school's reporting system, tracking students' engagement with learning habits (successful behaviour and routines associated with effective learning). Take a look at the data provided by the school below:

Year group	Round 1	Round 2	Difference
7	76.4	74.1	-2.3
8	73.6	77.4	3.8
9	70.3	71.8	1.5
10	68.7	69.5	0.8
11	70.6	72.6	2

Throughout 2022–23, there was particular focus on 'feed-forward' within teachers' pedagogy, which 'linked in training to pupils' learning habits around engaging with feedback', says Sam. 'This came through in our "reflection and improvement" learning habit. The data shows the average score for the "reflection and improvement" learning habit across Key Stages 3 and 4 (this is graded by four indicators, whereby all 1s, the top grade, would result in 100 per cent and all 4s, the bottom grade, would result in 0). Pupils' learning habits for all of the categories (classwork, homework, organisation, and reflection and improvement) are fed back to pupils and parents twice a year in their report.'

These outcomes demonstrate the year group's average grade from the first and second round, and in all but Year 7 there was an upward trend of pupils' habitual behaviours with regard to reflecting independently on their work.

TOOLKIT TIPS

Here are five ways you could ask 'feed-forward' questions. Ask students:

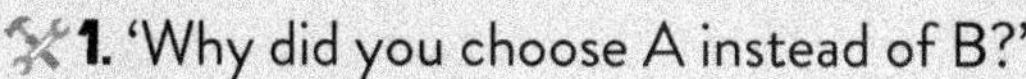

1. 'Why did you choose A instead of B?'

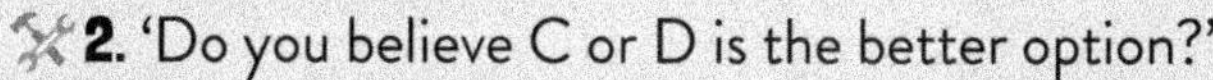

2. 'Do you believe C or D is the better option?'

3. 'How could you take your work one step forward?'

4. 'How do you know that this work is X grade?'

5. 'What grade do you think this is? Tell me one thing you need to do to reach the next level.'

In the next section of the book, we will walk through a worked example, inspired by academic research and the work of Kennet School.

WORKED EXAMPLE

One area of significant progress at Kennet School has been developing successful learning habits with students. One priority has been looking closely at 'reflection and improvement', where students are becoming more accustomed to seeking out misconceptions by themselves, rather than relying on the teacher, and more inclined to demonstrate an improved understanding of a topic. See the data in the table from Kennet School on page 71.

Sam Martin says, 'This has also filtered into our study mornings, where Key Stage 4 students use morning tutor time for revision. Tutors have reported that students are becoming increasingly independent and precise in their revision, identifying the recurring errors, and refining them for recall.'

To maximise your use of effective **verbal feed-forward**, you should begin with a clear learning objective and focus. In classrooms at Kennet School, staff have a clear sense of what they are looking for from students, **hunting out common misconceptions** rather than stumbling across them. They know what advice can enable students to feed-forward. This is often either a specific criterion, some content or a grammatical focus that provides a framework for the verbal advice. Specific advice:

1. What is the focus for using verbal feed-forward in any given context?
2. How is the information gained from students (checking for understanding) and moving them forward?
3. How do you quality-assure verbal feed-forward across all classrooms?
4. For consistency, how can you avoid any mutations of the original idea being lost in practice?
5. How do you support staff to gauge when to use verbal feed-forward versus other methods of feedback?

Scan to watch a video explanation of verbal feed-forward

In the next section, you can use a blank template to help to bring this concept to life.

TEMPLATE

Verbal feed-forward strategies

This template showcases different feed-forward strategies and prompts you can use with students.

Verbal feed-forward strategy	Prompt to use?	Student
Highlighting improvements	What one area could you improve?	
Linking feedback to learning objectives	How does this feedback relate to the learning goal?	
Encouraging self-assessment	Rate your understanding from 1–10.	
Using peer feedback	What advice would you give to another student on this task?	
Clarifying success criteria	What does success look like?	
Promoting reflective questioning	What would you do differently?	
Providing challenge without scaffolded support	How could you stretch this idea further?	
Providing challenge with scaffolded support	If you did A, B or C, do you think this would improve D or E?	
Encouraging application of feedback	How could you apply this information to your work?	

Scan to download a copy of the template

CHAPTER 7

NON-VERBAL FEEDBACK

Non-verbal feedback can be defined as body language and facial expressions that provide immediate, subtle feedback to students.
(Feedback = How am I going?)

Non-verbal (formative assessment) **feedback** is one of those strategies in classrooms that we often can take for granted. However, by being conscious of it, we can understand the power of (for example) gestures, facial cues and body language. Non-verbal feedback is subtle, but it can significantly impact how students perceive and respond to teacher instruction.

For example, a 'thumbs up', a nod or a smile can affirm correct answers or good effort, while a puzzled look, a glower or a 'hand wobble' can signal confusion or the need for improvement. In this chapter, we discuss how teachers can use **non-verbal feedback** to develop a positive learning environment, encourage participation and provide immediate feedback to students through the use of cues. In tandem with the school case study (from an independent school in Manchester), I will explain how you can develop a range of strategies to use 'on your feet' in the classroom, as well as how to evidence non-verbal feedback outside traditional quality assurance processes.

I will discuss not only how to use non-verbal feedback (the journey), but also when and why to use it, together with how it compares to non-verbal feed-up (comparison) and non-verbal feed-forward (explanation).

EXPLAINER

In 'Casting doubt on the old myth', Andersen and Andersen suggest that students respond positively to teachers who are warm, friendly and approachable (1987). These qualities lead to better teacher–student relationships and higher student satisfaction. More importantly, teachers who express positivity and care through verbal and non-verbal cues are perceived as more effective. This challenges the traditional view that strictness and emotional distance are necessary for classroom control and highlights the importance of positive emotional communication in teaching. Absolutely!

But how do teachers incorporate this into their practice?

Using **non-verbal** cues such as smiling, eye contact and a friendly tone to create a more inviting classroom atmosphere helps to embrace warmth and positive student interactions. According to Arnold, 'When students are given the opportunity to [regulate] their learning... make connections, and evaluate ideas in a safe and welcoming environment with their peers, their opportunities to succeed in the classroom and in life increase.' (2020, p. 5) This is also true in an online context in which keeping students engaged is challenging. Creating a welcoming environment is 'shown to improve not only retention among students but teach important skills necessary to learning' (Arnold, 2020, p. 5). It can add significant value!

When teachers demonstrate genuine interest and care in their students' progress and wellbeing, they lay the foundations for excellent classroom management. This fosters a sense of belonging and trust among students, mitigating defiance and unruly classroom behaviour. By cultivating a nurturing environment, and doing so consistently, teachers not only enhance students' engagement, but also develop long-term academic interest.

The key question for this chapter is: 'How can teachers achieve this physically?' What does **non-verbal feedback** look like? Here is a quick definition recap.

Non-verbal communication can be defined as body language and facial expressions that provide information to others in a classroom context, by supporting immediacy, workload and motivation. Remember, the definition of 'feedback' is reflecting on progress: 'How am I going?' This means any non-verbal feedback strategy we discuss or use must reflect on the progress completed to date. Our challenge here is: how do we teachers achieve this, and how do we provide a range of sources to suggest that this type of formative assessment adds value?

We will return to defining a range of outcomes in the last section of this chapter, but for now, let's clarify **what 'non-verbal' formative assessment is** and **is not** and how you can approach this as a 'feedback' classroom methodology.

What non-verbal feedback is:

Non-verbal formative strategies, especially those centred around feedback, are varied and can be subtly integrated into daily classroom interactions. Non-verbal gestures include:

1. **Thumbs up/down:** After explaining a concept, a teacher could ask students to show 'thumbs up' if they understand or 'thumbs down' if they don't. This quick check allows the teacher to gauge comprehension levels without interrupting the flow of the lesson. Equally, the teacher could reverse this and offer a thumbs up/down signal to a student when in verbal or non-verbal conversation. Many teachers will be able to recount a time when they have given this non-verbal gesture to a student from the other side of the classroom or playground! However, please be mindful of context and use discretion.

2. **Hand signals for self-assessment:** Teachers can use hand signals such as holding up a certain number of fingers to ask students to self-assess their confidence in a topic or task. For example, five fingers could mean 'very confident', while one finger might mean 'not confident at all'. Over time, this routine may become automated. It may also be worth you as the teacher explicitly making a note of responses. As soon as a teacher 'gestures' five fingers in the air, the students know what is coming next. Or you could perhaps make a triple-tap noise on the desk to connotate 'get ready to show the teacher'.

3. **Facial expressions for encouragement/concern:** Facial expressions are something we all take for granted. Nodding affirmatively when a student is on the right track, or showing concern through facial expressions when a student seems confused, can provide immediate non-verbal feedback that supports or redirects the student's learning process. We should all be mindful, however, when having conversations with students and teachers (or anyone in everyday life, for that matter) who are deaf or hard of hearing. In these situations, our facial gestures as well as our body positioning are important. You may have come across this during your teacher training.

4. **Proximity for silent monitoring and support:** Simply standing closer to a student who may be struggling can be a non-verbal indicator of support. This presence can encourage the student and subtly indicate that the teacher is available for help. Equally, when a student is off task, circulating around the room and pausing at that student's desk can be all it takes to help them get back on track. A simple hand gesture for 'What's going on?' (both palms held up, facing the sky) offers the student a non-verbal cue to get back to work. Equally, a student may feel able to initiate a question if the teacher is near, rather than feeling exposed by asking a question in front of the whole class. At this point, it may be appropriate to validate the student's question by saying that they have made a useful point and then sharing that useful point with the whole class. Other students may have been silently asking the same question but feeling awkward about asking it. This means that the teacher not only 'hears' the original student's question but also applauds them for asking it by sharing it with the others, i.e. 'Joe has raised an excellent point here about...'.
5. **Gestures to guide learning:** Gestures such as slowing down, speeding up or pausing conversations, or even body movements such as walking or leading a demonstration, can be used to communicate the pace at which teachers think students should be working, especially during independent or group tasks.
6. **Visual aids for clarification:** Using visual aids like charts or graphs and pointing to specific areas can provide non-verbal feedback that clarifies or emphasises certain points without verbal explanation. Showing an exemplar piece of work with a 'thumbs down' and an exemplar piece of work with a 'thumbs up' is a simple yet effective non-verbal indicator. It gives students direction on how to tackle a particular task.
7. **Miming actions for procedures or behaviour expectations:** Teachers can mime actions to remind students of the proper procedure (like miming the act of opening a book to a certain page) or expected behaviour (like putting a finger to lips to indicate the need for silence). We all use many of these cues already (perhaps more often than we are aware of) in our everyday lives; with conscious effort, these can be used effectively in the classroom.

What non-verbal feedback is not:

1. It is not a one-size-fits-all approach. For example, some students may find a certain gesture useful, while others don't.
2. It should not be used simply for correction or approval.
3. It is not a standalone feedback method. Non-verbal feedback can be misinterpreted, so it is important to explain what your cues mean so that you can use them in the future more effectively.
4. It is not universally understood by all students, so ensure your meaning has been successfully received.

Examples of non-verbal cues include:

1. **Nodding**: Shows agreement, understanding or encouragement.
2. **Shaking head**: Signals disagreement or disapproval.
3. **Raised eyebrows**: Shows surprise, curiosity or questioning.
4. **Frowning**: Expresses confusion, concern or disapproval.
5. **Smiling**: Indicates happiness, approval or a welcoming attitude.
6. **Eye contact**: Demonstrates attention, interest or focus.
7. **Crossed arms**: Can imply resistance, defensiveness or self-comfort.
8. **Leaning in**: Shows interest or engagement.
9. **Leaning back**: Indicates disengagement, shock (depending on speed) or surprise.
10. **Pointing**: Directs attention to a specific person, object or location.
11. **Waving hand**: Used for greeting, saying goodbye or drawing attention.
12. **Palms open and upward**: Signifies openness, honesty or submission.
13. **Thumbs up**: Generally means approval or that everything is good. This can sometimes be followed by a rotating hand gesture to say 'give me more information/keep going'.
14. **Thumbs down**: Indicates disapproval, disagreement or dislike.
15. **Tapping fingers**: Suggests impatience or for attention.

16. **Clapping hands**: Used to show appreciation, encouragement or agreement. Also excellent for gaining attention of the class.

17. **Rubbing chin or side of forehead**: Implies deep thinking or consideration.

18. **Hand on heart**: Suggests sincerity, gratitude or a pledge.

19. **Shrugging shoulders**: Indicates uncertainty, indifference or a lack of knowledge.

20. **Hands on hips**: Can imply readiness, assertiveness or frustration.

These non-verbal strategies not only add variety to feedback but also cater to the different needs of our students, particularly the most vulnerable, where silent cues offered across the room reduce any unwanted attention from peers. They can be particularly useful in maintaining a positive and engaged learning environment. However, it is worth bearing in mind – as the list above shows – that some non-verbal gestures have different meanings in different cultures or environments, or are open to interpretation, so ensure the student is clear about what your intended meaning is.

In the next section, we analyse **non-verbal feedback** strategies provided by **Withington Girls' School,** a leading independent day school in Manchester for girls aged seven to 18 years, who achieve some of the best academic results in the country. There are approximately 600 students in the senior school, with a diverse range of students attending from across the region. Students typically sit nine GCSEs and then attend the sixth form. About 15 per cent of students go on to study at either the University of Oxford or Cambridge.

PRACTICAL IDEA

Case study from Withington Girls' School: Feedback gestures

Any quoted material in this section comes from a case study provided by assistant headteacher Esther Suttle.

Non-verbal feedback (body language and facial expressions) that provides immediate, subtle feedback to students not only transforms outcomes, but is also a valuable and alternative source of formative assessment to use for quality assurance.

When I worked with the school staff at Withington Girls' School, I was really excited to see how far they had developed their formative assessment thinking. They were a perfect case study for this book! I wanted to know why **non-verbal feedback** was a particular strength at the school. Esther Suttle, assistant headteacher, said: 'Students at Withington respond positively to non-verbal feedback. It provides our students with guidance on their learning in real time. The students are motivated by their teachers' non-verbal feedback, which encourages and inspires their progress, providing confidence and independence of thought and task throughout each lesson.'

I then asked Esther how the school achieved this. She replied, 'The school has a small working party, which was established to look at **all** types of feedback. This led to interesting conversations about different ways of giving "real-time" feedback to students away from "traditional" methods of marking and feedback.' What I admire about Withington's approach is that a 'sub-group within the working party was tasked with collecting evidence about the ways that non-verbal feedback is used in school', with the student voice being a significant part of this work. From this, the school established more effective ways of providing students with feedback, 'making **non-verbal communication explicit** and **conscious** rather than simply implicit or unintentional'. Fantastic!

As we move into these last three chapters on non-verbal communication, the difficult question for all teachers is how this method can improve student outcomes. And how do you gather any evidence for quality assurance? Esther's response to this was that 'Withington students are engaged and attentive in lessons; the immediacy that non-verbal feedback provides means that students are receiving (conscious) non-verbal signals of information about their progress, regularly throughout lessons. Students can act on this independently without the flow of learning being lost.'

The school's sub-group evaluations suggested that students are enthusiastic about lessons that explicitly contain non-verbal feedback; their engagement in these lessons has increased. Similarly, their confidence to contribute to class discussions is supported by non-verbal feedback, as students receive cues from their teachers throughout the lesson to support how they are progressing. How do you evidence an increase in confidence?

Scan to see student responses during a group discussion

Students at Withington were 'keen to discuss non-verbal feedback with their teachers' and this opened up metacognitive conversations about how students were constantly refining their work and their thinking based on the immediate non-verbal feedback they were receiving. Esther says this internal quality assurance research has 'generated a profitable and enlightening pedagogical conversation with staff about the micro-decisions we all make in our classrooms'. Harnessing the power of non-verbal feedback has been highly effective for this school, prompting both staff and students to think about progress in lessons in an entirely different way. To what extent is your school achieving this?

TOOLKIT TIPS

1. Follow the recommendations from Withington Girls' School. Ask your teaching and learning team to discuss all nine types of formative assessment in the book. What areas do you still need to develop?

2. How could you establish two or three clear non-verbal cues to use in your classroom?

3. How would you combine these with your current verbal feedback methods? For example, as you deliver some positive commentary, what explicit non-verbal gesture could you always provide to the students?

4. What non-verbal cues could you use to help motivate disappointed students?

In the next section, I will walk you through a worked example of this technique.

WORKED EXAMPLE

Students should see and feel the positive affirmation they receive from their teachers during lessons. The most common example of types of non-verbal feedback is a 'thumbs up, which teachers use frequently to signal to students that their ideas and contributions are accurate'.

While this seems like a small thing, the benefits are numerous:

1. The flow of the lesson is not lost.
2. Feedback is given without interruption.
3. Positive communication happens silently.
4. Students receive more feedback at regular intervals.

During periods of live assessment, teachers should circulate the classroom, providing 'thumbs up' to those doing well. These students then have the confidence to continue to work independently in the same vein. This frees up the teacher to work with students who require more thorough support (for example, feed-up or feed-forward). Students who have not been provided with a 'thumbs up' at a particular point know that there are elements of their work that could be improved.

When the teacher provides an intervention, the teacher can suggest some options for the student to take the required action. Esther says, 'Another useful technique at this stage is to point to the part of the student's work/answer that could be improved', positioning the students to 'take ownership of their progress and improvement'. Similarly, the signal to 'keep going' or to 'add more detail' is also used frequently and to great effect.

During discussion, these cues are used to prompt students to add to their responses without the teacher needing to interrupt the class. This approach stretches students to think beyond their initial responses, supporting the development of critical thinking skills and more thoughtful responses. Students reported to Withington's working party that they felt 'comforted and encouraged' by this approach and, as a result, more (conscious) live non-verbal feedback is being used around the school. Fantastic!

To apply these ideas to your school or classroom, I would recommend classroom positioning as a very effective form of non-verbal feedback to start with. Teachers position themselves next to particular students when they are asking for silence or attention; students are astute at picking up on these non-verbal signals and often modify their attention and work ethic as a result. This 'positioning' can be paired with signals like fingers on lips, raised eyebrows, tapping the desk or pointing at the page or the board to redirect student focus.

Starting your school's conversation about where and how non-verbal feedback is already happening in your classroom is key. How to evaluate and evidence these methods and their impact on student outcomes will require some detailed thought. Once your school is ready to take this next step, Esther says, 'student confidence and independence increases, and the teacher's capacity to offer more feedback throughout a lesson increases'. As a result, teacher workload decreases and the school's ability to evidence a more varied range of outcomes grows.

TEMPLATE

Planning different gestures and cues

This template will help you plan gestures for different situations, to assist you in the process of establishing non-verbal cues with your class.

How would you evaluate these varied gestures and cues that teachers provide in their classrooms every day? If teachers were using these explicitly as teaching routines in their classrooms, what impact would it have on behaviour management or teaching and learning? How do you evidence that a specific technique you used – not observed by others in the moment – could be demonstrably linked to student outcomes? For example, participation in lesson, completion of work or reward points, to name a few sources of evidence.

Take a look at the template and scribble in your thoughts in the right-hand column. If you experimented with each stage, how do your students respond? How much time do you think you should dedicate to teaching them how to respond?

Stage	What to do?	Your example (add notes)
Establish non-verbal communication cues you will use	Spend some time with your class explaining your top three cues. For example: 1) Wait 2) Get ready 3) Listen	
Reinforce positive behaviours	During a class discussion, how could you keep the conversation moving but signal to a student that their contribution was excellent?	
Address any misconceptions	What exemplar work could you have to hand as an excellent example so that you can use this alongside a non-verbal feedback gesture?	
Seek clarification	A student hesitates to answer a question or provide an explanation. What gesture could you use here to encourage them to speak up?	
Encourage peer-assessment	A student finishes their work early and you notice another student struggling. How could you encourage one student to help the other? What non-verbal gestures could you use?	
Behaviour management	The class are running out of time to complete an activity. What non-verbal gesture could you use that can be seen across the classroom to indicate that the activity is about to end?	

Scan to download a copy of the template

CHAPTER 8

NON-VERBAL FEED-UP

Non-verbal feed-up can be defined as gestures and visual cues that set and reinforce learning goals and expectations non-verbally.
(Feed-up = Where am I going?)

Non-verbal feed-up involves gestures or visual aids that help to clarify learning goals or standards. Remember, **feed-up** (where am I going?) is when a teacher provides a **comparison** of the actual status of the new piece of work produced to the **current target status** of the student. The challenge is how to do this non-verbally. For example, pointing to the highest point on a chart or graph could symbolise high expectations or targets. Alternatively, a teacher could take a look at a student's piece of work, give a 'hand wobble' and then direct the student to 'look up' by gesturing with a finger pointing towards one of the classroom displays that models some exemplar pieces of work.

The teacher could provide a non-verbal 'come here' hand gesture, encouraging the student to leave their seat and approach the other side of the classroom. The teacher would then point to the grade or a piece of work to let the student know that this is their target grade, and this is what they should be working towards. The teacher may also point to a specific piece of assessment to guide the student. There may be a short exchange of words to make the current assessment point clear. So, there are many things you can do!

Secondly, if **non-verbal feed-up** is a tried-and-tested technique in your institution, how do you evidence this alongside traditional quality assurance processes, where school and college leaders, parents and inspectors check up on teachers' marking and insist that all feedback is written down? In this chapter, I will look at how our case study school demonstrates ways in which this can be achieved, especially in supporting some of the most vulnerable students in our education system. The case study school, for example, helps its students to improve their social skills.

In summary, non-verbal feed-up can be a powerful tool for setting the tone for learning, conveying expectations without words and reinforcing verbal messages about goals and objectives. It can also be a very powerful motivational tool for students, so when learned and implemented well, it can be a useful pedagogical technique. It also alleviates teachers' workload when promoted as an explicit teacher technique to use (other than marking books).

EXPLAINER

In this section, I will provide a range of non-verbal summaries of available educational research that can be adapted into your classroom practice. At the time of writing, the DfE has announced that students across the English education system will be able to study a GCSE in British Sign Language (BSL), 'recognised in law as a language of Great Britain in the BSL Act 2022 (DfE, 2023b)'. This is fantastic news!

Throughout my teaching career, I have taught partially deaf students and recently worked with some trainee teachers who are deaf. This experience makes you think very carefully about how you present yourself, communicate and transfer information.

The government have said, 'Students will be taught at least 750 signs and how to use them to communicate effectively with other signers for use in work, social and academic settings.' (DfE, 2023b)

According to the British Deaf Association (BDA, n.d.), sign language is 'the preferred language of over 87,000 deaf people in the UK'. I am curious about how people who experience deafness communicate non-verbally, and I believe there is much wisdom that we, as teachers, can gain from these practices, particularly in terms of how we unconsciously use non-verbal gestures to communicate every day in the classroom.

According to the 2023 report from the Consortium for Research into Deaf Education (CRIDE), the number of deaf children in England is 45,671. In published BDA research in 2012, there were at least '34,927 (reported) deaf children in England, but only 9 per cent use sign language to some extent to communicate' (BDA, 2012, p. 19). This figure is surprisingly low.

Understanding the nuances of non-verbal communication, such as the significance of a teacher's posture, facial expressions and gestures, can be crucial in the classroom. We can learn numerous lessons from the people in our daily lives who communicate non-verbally. These transferable gestures would be especially useful for teachers in the classroom.

Now, let's explore a range of gestures, and I will explain how non-verbal cues can bridge communication gaps and provide clear expectations for students.

In our classrooms, non-verbal signals usually go **unrecognised**, especially when evaluating quality and reliability. We all know they hold huge potential for communication. In the research 'Role of non verbal communication in improving quality of teaching learning process', Ahuja digs into the multifaceted role of non-verbal cues in the classroom, offering interesting insights into **non-verbal communication components** (2010). Some I was familiar with but others were entirely new to me, which is why I wanted to share them with you.

Kinesics

'Kinesics' (non-verbal signals) are gestures, facial expressions and postures that can significantly reinforce expectations and understanding. Examples include 'shrugs, foot tapping, drumming fingers, eye movements [such as], winking, facial expressions'. These signpost some of the cues we might make throughout the day to others and 'can be a step towards assessing engagement and understanding' (Ahuja, 2010, p. 4).

Proxemics and proximity

'Proximity' is a term we are all familiar with, but 'proxemics' refers to the amount of space someone feels is necessary between themselves and the person they are communicating with. Proximity is significant when it comes to student safeguarding, and it is also relevant in terms of cultural or religious norms, which 'dictate a comfortable distance for interaction with [a] student' (Ahuja, 2010, p. 4). Practically speaking, this could be, for example, a slight lean-in to signify that you are listening carefully or that you want the student to take the conversation a little more seriously – but without encroaching on their personal space. This is a handy top tip when managing behaviour!

Haptics

'Haptics' is a term I have been familiar with for over 15 years, something I first understood when I worked alongside headteacher Paul Sutton OBE in Tottenham, North London. Paralysed from the neck down, Paul cannot use his hands and therefore cannot use the (haptic) touch features on mobile phone screens. The research suggests that haptics is a physical cue 'projected by the instructor [to] communicate a message to students' (Ahuja, 2010, p. 4). Taking your school's safeguarding policy into account, and always erring on the side of caution and avoiding physical contact if you are not absolutely sure, you may feel there are times when a pupil will benefit from haptics as a non-verbal gesture to communicate. It is vital, however, to take into account the age and gender of the pupil, your relationship with them, the context it happens in, and anything else you know is an important safeguarding consideration before you do this, and always err on the side of not doing it unless you are certain. One example might be congratulating an older pupil you know well in a more informal context, such as a sports match, by giving them a brief pat on the back for a job well done. This type of non-verbal feedback, however, is certainly to be used sparingly, due to safeguarding concerns.

Other non-verbal components include:

1. **Oculesics:** Eye contact to help regulate the flow of communication.
2. **Chronemics:** How we perceive and use time to affect communication. For example, I could provide you with immediate or delayed feedback, depending on the context of your work, your motivation, self-esteem and the nature of the assessment.
3. **Paralanguage:** Pitch, speed and sounds (e.g. groans and huffs and puffs).
4. **Posture:** How to physically position yourself in the classroom in order to manage behaviour, have private conversations or mirror approachable behaviours.
5. **Appearance:** Teacher characteristics may impact student outcomes. 'Individuals with high levels of emotional stability are calm, secure, and tolerant of stress.' (John et al., 2008) How do we present ourselves and how does our appearance have an effect on others? Whether it is an unconscious bias or not, your height, body shape, body odour, hair and perceived attractiveness to others are all non-verbal influences. As a male teacher who is well over six feet tall, it was rare that I was threatened, but it did happen; however, another person may have more frequent experiences than me. Now, take a moment to reflect on other teachers you work with who have different physical characteristics. How does this influence how they teach and the way in which students respond to them?
6. **Artifacts:** Our clothing, tattoos and jewellery communicate personal identity. We should also consider objects used in the classroom, such as red, amber and green flashcards inside student planners, as another example of non-verbal communication.

All of the above are relevant when reflecting on how we use non-verbal signals in our everyday lives. So, why should this be any different in the classroom? Are these techniques in your school or college undervalued when it comes to 'feedback' and quality assurance processes?

Let's switch to the 'feed-up' aspects of all of the aforementioned. Remember, 'feed-up' means 'where am I going?' and aims to **explain** and **reinforce learning goals** and **expectations**, and how to reach them.

How do we implement these non-verbal methods as a 'feed-up' formative assessment strategy?

I think it's important to consider that feed-up doesn't always have to relate to learning goals. The definition also relates to expectations, and nothing is more important than using non-verbal cues to manage behavioural expectations.

In *Nonverbal Communication*, a book unpicking 'what research says to the teacher', Miller suggests that 'teachers should be aware of non-verbal communication in the classroom for two reasons:

1. To become better receivers of student messages.
2. To gain the ability to send students positive signals.' (1986)

Just as students nod their heads or put their thumbs up to gesture that they have understood the teacher, teachers themselves should become familiar with non-verbal communication 'to become better message senders'.

In the next section of this chapter, you will discover **non-verbal feed-up** strategies used by **Leaways School**, an independent co-educational school in London for 60 students aged seven to 18 years. The school supports students who cannot continue in mainstream education and have a range of different educational needs, including ASD, attention deficit hyperactivity disorder (ADHD) and social, emotional and mental health (SEMH) needs.

PRACTICAL IDEA

Case study from Leaways School: Objective cues

Any quoted material in this section comes from a case study provided by James Hinton.

Non-verbal feed-up can support students' wellbeing and other outcomes, such as attendance and punctuality: another valuable source of evidence for quality assurance purposes.

Non-verbal feed-up is a particular strength at Leaways School because students with special educational needs benefit from non-verbal gestures to stay on task. For example, 'teachers point two fingers to their eyes' and then 'gesture down with one finger'. This cue signals students to keep on task and maintain high expectations. There are many non-verbal feed-up gestures that the school uses in order to correct behaviour in a non-confrontational way. This helps, says James Hinton, to maintain 'our teachers' positive relationships with our students. An effective non-verbal gesture also ensures that other students aren't distracted from their work.'

Scan to watch a short demonstration of a non-verbal gesture

At Leaways School, the team have effectively used non-verbal feed-up by working as a team to achieve consistency. This has been supported by training workshops to share collaborative teaching approaches or sharing constructive feedback from lesson observations. The school works hard to create an environment that allows staff to reflect on their practice – for example, how a non-verbal gesture may have been a more effective method of feedback than singling out an individual student in front of their peers. Students with special educational needs at Leaways School benefit from consistency, so the staff have worked to develop key non-verbal gestures and cues to use with the students to improve behaviour for learning. As a result, engagement in lessons has improved.

Scan to see an example of how these techniques have improved school outcomes and how to evidence this

Technology also plays a key role in boosting student engagement. The students use tablets, laptops, robotic LEGO™ and virtual reality headsets in lessons. The school states that using non-verbal feed-up gestures has improved student outcomes. James Hinton says that 'we have found the use of non-verbal gestures has significantly improved behaviour', with better redirection to tasks, 'achieved more effectively through a simple gesture'. As students' social skills improve, the quality and completion of written work have also improved.

In a SEMH setting, students being guided back to work in a non-confrontational and consistent way is very likely to have a positive impact. When schools and colleges consider how a teacher can use non-verbal assessment in the classroom using explicit techniques, they can also learn how to evidence its impact elsewhere. For example, at Leaways School, James Hinton says there has been a 'significant improvement in attendance, fewer behavioural incidents in lessons and improved attainment'.

Scan for an example of how non-verbal feedback is monitored with students in class

So what do these non-verbal feed-up gestures look like in practice?

1. **Positioning:** All schools should reward 'good behaviour' whenever it is seen. This is especially important in a school setting such as Leaways School. Non-verbal gestures, often subconscious, can easily be taken for granted. At Leaways School, 'the staff have done a lot of work to ensure teachers position themselves in the most effective place in the classroom', close enough to students where explicit non-verbal modelling can have an impact, allowing the teacher to give positive reinforcement and correct any undesirable behaviour in a non-verbal, non-confrontational way.

2. **Hand gestures:** Teachers can use a huge range of gestures, and different gestures will work for different teachers, students, subjects and scenarios. Below are some non-verbal cues that Leaways School have used consistently:
   - **Thumbs up:** Used to reinforce the positive behaviour and effort of the student.
   - **Open palm slightly raised in a 'Stop' gesture:** Used to address unwanted behaviour in a non-confrontational way.
   - **Signing your hand (similar to 'writing'):** Used to encourage a student to start working in a non-confrontational way.
   - **Pointing at eyes and then at the student's work:** Used to redirect students' attention back to their current task.

Other non-verbal feed-up ideas that **reinforce learning goals and expectations** include:

- **Index finger to lips** as a gesture for quiet.
- **A letter T shape** with both forefingers to indicate a pause or time out.
- **Tapping the wrist** with a forefinger to signal time up or hurry up.
- **Pointing at a student and then to the door** to signal to a student that they have permission to leave.
- **Nodding** or **crossed arms** to signal pleasure or frustration.

All teachers will use a mixture of the above gestures in the classroom and some schools may have an agreed set of gestures or an approach that teachers should use. If not, then this may be something your school or college may want to consider, to support teaching and learning.

Scan to view the school's teaching and learning policy

Drawing upon some of the work from Leaways School, **how could other teachers and schools apply some of their ideas within their context?** 'Non-verbal gestures offer an excellent opportunity to re-engage students', says James Hinton. Using facial and body gestures explicitly, particularly in a non-confrontational way, can motivate students, especially vulnerable students. They add so much value across the classroom space, used in micro-silent moments between the teacher and the student. Gestures can provide an immediate and impactful way to ensure the lesson moves on smoothly. Students can receive the affirmation (or not) that they need to move forward in the learning process.

As we have seen in the Leaways School example, I would recommend other schools and colleges start with the following:

1. Add this topic into staff training sessions.
2. Define what 'feed-up' looks like in different subjects.
3. Develop a simple diagram of rules and expectations in lessons for teachers to use.
4. Film and document teachers learning how to position themselves in the classroom.
5. Consciously evaluate a toolkit of hand gestures that students are familiar with, and consider how these cues add value.

WORKED EXAMPLE

Let's consider a classroom scenario where a teacher walks through rows of students engrossed in their work and then approaches a student struggling with the concept of electric circuits.

1. The teacher approaches the student and catches their gaze. The student looks up with a frown across their forehead, with an incomplete circuit on the table.
2. Recognising the problem, the teacher 'leans in' to offer reassurance. Using a red-laser pointer, the teacher points across to the front of the classroom to a completed circuit diagram on the whiteboard.
3. The teacher 'points' with their forefinger on the student's classwork to the broken section of the student's circuit, then 'tilts their head to the side' with a look here (eye gesture) to indicate to the student to look towards the whiteboard.
4. The teacher then circles a section of the whiteboard with their red laser pen while tapping the student's (broken) circuit board. At this stage, not a single word is spoken.
5. The teacher steps back, which is a cue for the student to take the lead.
6. The student picks up a resistor and a wire, before deciding that the resistor must be the missing component that needs to be connected to the circuit.
7. The student makes the connection and the bulb lights up. The student then 'clenches both fists' on the desk to mark a small victory.
8. The student looks up, and in a millisecond, the teacher offers a 'slight nod' with an 'encouraging smile'.
9. The teacher walks off to assist another student. The teacher's immediate departure signals that this small victory has nothing to do with how they have communicated with the student; rather, that the student has used the cues to achieve the desired outcome.

How many small non-verbal events like this happen in classrooms up and down the country? Often unobserved, this valuable teaching moment, non-verbal feed-up, shows how teachers can intervene **to reinforce learning goals and expectations**.

This example interaction is never monitored in work scrutiny or data collection trawls, and this is why we must be better at knowing what goes on in our classrooms and develop a broader view of outcomes. How can we document small teaching moments like this? With parent permission, examples could be captured on video. QR codes could be used as a quick way of accessing these during open evenings, professional development sessions or curriculum discussions. However, although the video catcher is great for professional development, it shouldn't be a mechanism used purely to evidence that it is happening. Going back to my point about outcomes, how do we evidence that teachers are doing these things to a high quality and that we can see the differences in student outcomes (defined by great behaviour, for example, or completing the circuit!)?

What if we defined formative assessment not just by a grade but also by reviewing student attendance and punctuality? If students love their lessons, they are more likely to show up! What about good staff attendance? If teachers enjoy working with their students, they won't become anxious about particular students or times in the week when they are working with a particular class. We could also consider subject admissions. If students love earlier experiences with teachers and their subjects, they may go on to study it further. A high uptake at GCSE options or on courses at college would be a strong indicator of success. Overall, non-verbal gestures add significant value to student motivation and outcomes, beyond simply a grade. How you demonstrate this evidence will need some thought.

TEMPLATE

Reflecting on objective cues

I hope the following template will help you to analyse the strategies you currently use. Remember, feed-up is a signpost to your students about a point in time, comparing current work to expected progress. Doing this non-verbally will be a challenge, but not impossible. Consider how facial gestures and hand signals can be used in proximity to your students.

This template is offered to help you reflect on the current non-verbal techniques and cues you use, and those that you need to develop further.

Strategy	Examples of what this looks like	What do you currently do?
Appearance	Dressing professionally for the relevant role to set an example	
Artifacts	Using visual aids like flashcards	
Body language	Open arms Folded arms Slouched Puffed chest	
Chronemics	Using time effectively, like timing tasks E.g. timer on whiteboard display	
Eye contact	Fleeting look Prolonged look Looking between the student and their work	
Facial expressions	Smile Eyebrow lift Wide eyes 'Wow' mouth expression	
Gestures	Thumbs up or down Head tilt	

Haptics	Handshake Pat on the back for a job well done	
Kinesics	Shrugs Foot tapping Drumming fingers Winking	
Oculesics	Maintaining eye contact to regulate communication flow	
Paralanguage	Varying pitch Speed of talking Using sounds like 'sighs'	
Proximity	Lean in Stand close by Take a step back Facing the student(s) Not facing the student(s) At the other side of the room	
Posture	Standing straight to show confidence Slouching Folded arms Legs apart, chin up	

Scan to download a copy of the template

CHAPTER 9

NON-VERBAL FEED-FORWARD

Non-verbal feed-forward is defined as using non-verbal signals to guide students towards future actions or learning strategies.
(Feed-forward = Where to next?)

In this chapter, we consider **non-verbal feed-forward**, which might include gestures that suggest action or direction, such as pointing or guiding a student to the next step in the learning process. Remember that feed-forward includes an explanation of what a student should **do next** to reach their target status, based on their actual status of the work. How do you do this using non-verbal gestures?

One way of doing this is to model behaviours or strategies that students could emulate in future tasks. For example, if you 'rotate both hands' from side to side underneath your chin, you would be gesturing that someone needs to fix their tie. Or you might gesture to a student across the classroom by pointing four fingers (in a square) of one hand down onto the palm of your other hand to indicate that they need to put all four legs of their chair down on the floor to avoid having an accident. Another example includes signalling to a student by opening your mouth and pointing into it to tell the student non-verbally to empty their mouth or spit out their chewing gum.

Non-verbal feed-forward can be particularly effective for low-level behaviour management, but also for showing students how to apply skills and knowledge in classroom scenarios, especially during demonstrations. In my experience, working in a very noisy design technology workshop, with perhaps 20 or 30 students in the room who are all using machinery, can be an incredibly noisy environment. In these types of situations, you should be acutely aware of your body position, keeping sight of all the students in the room. You may periodically need to work with one or two individuals at a time, but you will nevertheless need to listen actively to the sounds of the machines and tools at work, spotting any unusual activity to keep all students safe. The same type of scenario could apply to a school laboratory or PE sports hall. Our learning environment is crucial to who we are and how we live and work.

I've also learned on my teacher training travels, working with specialist schools and vulnerable students, that there is a whole range of pedagogical techniques used methodically by teachers to gesture to students about what they should do next. It is a fascinating world!

EXPLAINER

We have now established that **non-verbal** communication is defined as using gestures or signals to guide students towards future actions or learning strategies. **Feed-forward ('where to next?')** helps the student focus on how to resolve current problems. Feed-forward, by definition, should come with an explanation, so the challenge here is how to do this non-verbally?!

To help support students, as mentioned in Chapter 1, it is important to explicitly teach them metacognitive strategies (that is, knowledge of themselves, knowledge of the task and strategies available to solve the problem), in order to support them towards regulating their own learning and thinking critically.

In Malik's study, 'A study on the impact of non-verbal communication of secondary teachers on their classroom students' (2023), which involved 30 students and ten teachers, it was suggested that non-verbal elements in the classroom, especially a secondary classroom, are limited. Yet techniques such as facial expressions and body language play an important role in shaping students' perceptions and motivation and the classroom atmosphere. 'Despite the presence of these non-verbal components in classrooms by good teachers, their use was not optimal.' (Malik, 2023, p. 30) The paper reminds us that teaching involves a lot more than just speaking, and how teachers use non-verbal cues, such as body language, expressions and gestures, has an impact. Malik suggests that teachers:

1. would benefit from using non-verbal cues to create a livelier atmosphere in class
2. should use non-verbal cues to enhance learning
3. who use facial expressions can command attention
4. who use students' non-verbal cues adapt their teaching effectively.

Effective classroom techniques require awareness about how they should be used and how students are expected to respond. For example, if I did a clap-clap, clap-clap in quick succession with my hands, students would become aware that this is a routine I use to control classroom behaviour. Therefore, over time, when students are asked to be quiet, they will repeat back the double clap-clap to me in order to help us to move forward with the lesson.

By spending a little bit of time training the students in how to respond to our strategies, we can save time on our workload overall. This also helps students develop a degree of self-regulation for their learning.

Non-verbal cues, when used effectively, can be a powerful tool to support the learning process, but can also support student wellbeing and mental health. According to Couper, who explored working with students who are non-verbal, technology also has 'benefits of improving functional communication for students who have been unable to communicate their needs' (2015, p. 209). For my master's degree, a long time ago, I explored the use of technology and semiotics in my classroom-based research.

The research concludes that video-recorded presentations can improve students' learning – and **feed-forward** skills in particular: 'By encouraging the development of metacognitive awareness, this assessment task provided students with significant feed-forward information for oral presentation tasks.' (Murphy and Barry, 2015, p. 224) Students gain more from the assessment by gaining a deeper self-reflection. 'Many seem to believe that the more of these [grade predictions] we put in the records (Management Information System), the better the teaching will become.' (Nuthall, 2001, p. 22) Developing the learner's ability to act on information they receive (feed-forward), rather than on a grade they receive, *may* appear to have more benefit to learning. It is important for students undertaking peer-learning activities to be well prepared for providing and acting on appropriate and relevant feedback (Chan and Leijten, 2014). The conclusion? Teachers must invest not just in teaching students material, but in how to understand the assessment criteria, and plan, monitor and evaluate their progress against it.

Inspired by Chan and Leitjen's research, an analysis of the differences between feedback, feed-up and feed-forward is provided below. I will be the teacher (Mr McGill) and you (the reader) will be a student in my Year 7 food technology class.

Conversation	Assessment type	Comments
Mr McGill: That's a large amount of flour you are adding to your pizza dough.	Feed-up	Ross checks with you (the student) to find out why you have added too much flour to your recipe.

You: Yes, I'm happy with my recipe.	Feedback	You explain that you are happy with your choice, even though it is wrong.
Mr McGill: I am watching to see how this turns out in this lesson. I will pop back in a moment, once I have finished my demonstration with this group (points across room).	Feed-up	The teacher offers you a non-threatening gesture to check your progress.
You: Thanks, Mr McGill. I will come over and ask you for help in a moment.	Feedback	You check your recipe and look at other students in your group. You think 30 seconds of watching Mr McGill will help you check whether you are doing it right.
Mr McGill: So, this is how you make sure your pizza dough is just right so that it isn't too dry and doesn't burn on the base. Is everyone watching? (Offers a non-verbal 'nod' in your direction...)	Feed-up	There is an agreement between students watching the demonstration that the right amount of flour and water ensures the pizza dough is sticky enough to shape, and remains moist enough to cook without burning.
You: (Back at your desk) Mr McGill, do you think my dough is better now?	Feed-up	You seek a grade assessment in time about your progress. This could be written, verbal or non-verbal.
Mr McGill: Well, compared to your last attempt, this looks like the right consistency (places clean hand into the dough and stretches it). Do you think the consistency is good?	Feed-up	The teacher returns back to you after a worked example, checking for understanding, adapting teaching in the moment and providing a prompt to move you further forward.

You: It looks good, Sir. I think I'm ready to roll out the dough and add my ingredients.	Feedback	You confirm to the teacher what your decisions are and you signpost to the teacher how to assess your work at this time.
Mr McGill: (Leaning in as a motivational gesture) I think your pizza could be one of the best in the class this week. (Smiles in a friendly way and raises one eyebrow with both hands open to the ceiling, saying in a jokey manner) I wonder whether you will be cautious in your ingredients, or just throw everything on the top?	Feed-forward	The teacher does not waste an opportunity to keep you engaged, motivated and always learning. There are lots of non-verbal cues offered in this short moment, but there is a pivotal feed-forward moment to encourage you with your plan, and to monitor and evaluate your decisions. The teacher places their preferences to one side, and thinks carefully about the assessment criteria.

(adapted from Chan and Leijten, 2014, p. 27)

The brilliant **West London College** is the case study school for this chapter. It is a further education setting with three campuses for students (aged 16 to 18 years) with provision for adult learners (aged 19+) and those with high needs. Seven per cent of students are White British, with the majority from BAME (Black, Asian and minority ethnic) groups. Over 87 per cent of students are on provision at Level 2 and below.

PRACTICAL IDEA

Case study from West London College: Signal-act-confirm

Any quoted material in this section comes from a case study provided by assistant principal Sabeena Shah.

At West London College, 'We understand the importance of feedback to instil confidence in our learners, especially as we ensure learners are reaching the high-end jobs and course progression that they desire,' says Sabeena Shah, assistant principal for quality and the learner experience.

The college has embedded the importance of establishing regular feedback to learners in lessons and during their pastoral support sessions. Ninety-seven per cent of all learners said in their recent survey that they feel supported and receive regular feedback. The college has implemented a strict rule of feedback to feed-forward at least three times during the session. This can be either as a whole group or to individual learners.

Non-verbal communication helps to create a positive classroom environment and build strong relationships. Staff development sessions at the college ensure feed-forward is a particular **achievement** in classrooms.

Across the college, teachers focus on diverse feed-forward methods to support students, integrating non-verbal communication techniques into classroom practices. They 'ensure all students feel understood and valued, and we achieve this through understanding their individual needs and having targeted intervention plans that build on feedback'.

Using practical **non-verbal feed-forward methods has improved student outcomes**, improving retention rates for students where English is not their first language, evidenced by improving student attendance and participation. For instance, the majority of their English for speakers of other languages (ESOL) learners remain enrolled throughout their courses and report that they feel supported by their tutor and are on track to achieve.

Creating non-verbal feed-forward methods can help teachers to guide students through future actions effectively. Here are two examples:

1. Non-verbal feed-forward loop: Signal-act-confirm

Signal: The teacher uses a specific gesture to indicate to the student that a task has started or to highlight the focus area, such as looking carefully at a particular piece of text within an article. The teacher uses their hands to focus attention on a specific part of the article, using directional cues (finger rotating in a circle) to point towards resources or areas where the student should focus their efforts.

Act: The students engage in the task, looking carefully at the indicated area the teacher has signposted. The teacher circulates the classroom using non-verbal gestures like 'thumbs up' or 'nodding', but to ensure feed-forward is offered, the teacher has exemplar work on the whiteboard at the front of the class and also a completed worksheet in their hands.

Confirm: As the teacher moves around the room, they gesture with their hands, and circle the correct area of the work where each student should focus on next. When students appear to have resolved their next steps, the teacher can offer any number of confirmatory gestures to the student, in near or far proximity in the classroom – for example, a mini (silent) round of applause with both their hands in the air, delivered from the other side of the classroom. Alternatively, a 'fist bump' or 'hand shake' works well in close proximity as they walk past the student.

So, how would you evidence this excellent practice for quality assurance, away from the eyes of classroom observers?

In a second example, visual goal-setting is an effective way to communicate expectations.

2. Visual goal-setting

Using this technique allows the teacher to non-verbally communicate expectations towards the next stage of learning. How can you help to explain this assessment action to students without speaking?

Development: At the start of the year, the teacher developed with students a set of symbols to indicate how to interpret feedback, as well as a set of actions the student could take depending on the assessment received. You can see what this looks like in the worked example (page 111).

Application: These symbols are permanently on display in the classroom, plus students have a student-friendly version inside their exercise books. When the teacher provides any written, verbal or non-verbal assessment, there is often a reference by the teacher to these symbols during any form of communication with the student. This includes non-verbally pointing or highlighting with a circle or highlighter pen the current assessment point, and what the student should consider to improve their work ('Where to next?').

Reflection: Students are regularly invited to reflect on their progress by moving a small sticker marker inside their exercise book, perhaps along a progess line or up and down like a point on a graph. The purpose of this exercise is to align with their perceived progress, including against the teacher's current judgement. Another symbol could be offered to indicate the target that students are expected to reach.

Scan to see how a teacher sets non-verbal feed-forward goals at West London College

Your school or college can apply these approaches by identifying what you currently use, or using the above ideas and the template on page 115 as an idea. Other ideas you could explore include crib sheets, self-evaluation documents and tick-box matrices to allow students to self-assess progress against future targets.

TOOLKIT TIPS

1. Use visual aids to support non-verbal gestures.
2. Align these gestures with learning goals.
3. Develop a consistent set of non-verbal cues that you and your students understand; consider how they can be used across the organisation.
4. Actively model non-verbal feed-forward during lessons.

WORKED EXAMPLE

While looking at the template in the next section, bear in mind that non-verbal gestures are to guide students, and that feed-forward helps take students towards future actions or learning strategies. The template can help you to plan, implement and reflect on the current non-verbal feed-forward methods you use (or not) in your classroom. Don't forget to invest enough time on the implementation phase, which means training your students how to interpret the symbols. This will ultimately reduce your workload and help to empower all the students in front of you to regulate their learning.

Step 1: Implementing non–verbal feed-forward strategies

1. **Strategy selection:** Choose the non-verbal feed-forward ideas you would like to implement (for example, signal-act-confirm or visual goal-setting – see pages 109–110).
2. **Signal description:** Describe the specific non-verbal signals you will use.
3. **Action required:** Detail the action students are expected to take when receiving the non-verbal signal.
4. **Confirmation cues:** List the non-verbal gestures for confirming students' correct understanding or completion of the action (for example, a thumbs up).
5. **Visual aids:** If you consider having a poster display, think about the symbols or visual aids to be used, whether they can be accessed by all students visually across the classroom, and how they can be universally received by all students, regardless of age, stage or access.

Step 2: Implementing and reflecting on non-verbal feed-forward strategies

1. **Implementation:** Make a note in any curriculum plans, allowing you to understand how non-verbal feed-forward strategies will be used and where.
2. **Student responses:** Reflect on how students receive non-verbal feed-forward, and make adjustments in real time.

3. **Adjustments:** Reflect on the effectiveness of non-verbal feed-forward methods and plan any future adjustments to your curriculum. How do you know whether your methods are working? What difference do they make to student outcomes?

4. **Quality assurance:** Beyond classroom observation, how could your non-verbal communications be evidenced in your quality assurance methods currently used across the school/college? What other methods could you use? Imagine if your communications are being well received by students. What would a classroom survey tell you about their effectiveness?

This starting framework will give you something to think about. Feedback has traditionally been evidenced in teaching, and quality assurance is often sourced in 'deep dives' through lesson observation, work scrutiny and data analysis of past, current and predicted grades, or taking a look through students' exercise books, as well as occasionally having a conversation with the teacher and students.

The following table outlines some quality assurance methods you could use to evaluate other aspects of impact in your classroom. If your non-verbal strategies are working, it will also help you evidence them in quality assurance procedures.

Source of impact on student outcomes	How to quality-assure this outcome?
Student engagement	Track any changes in classroom engagement, such as increased hand-raising, participation in discussions or proactive questions posed by students, as indicators of effectiveness of non-verbal feed-forward.
Behaviour	Monitor any shifts in student behaviour. Note any reductions in behaviour events logged into a management information system, including increases or decreases in detention logs, phone calls home or notes in planners.
Attendance/ punctuality	Evaluate trends in student attendance before and after introducing non-verbal feed-forward strategies. Have any methods improved punctuality to lessons (for individuals or groups of students)?

Rewards and sanctions	Are there any notable differences in rewards or sanctions during or after non-verbal feed-forward strategies being explicitly introduced and used in lessons? To draw any reliable conclusions, you may want to have a control and a sample class, and determine a fixed period of time over which to use these methods.
Peer and self-assessment	Ask students to reflect on the clarity and effectiveness of the non-verbal cues that they receive from their teacher. Students should understand the verbal cues that teachers have been using, so that they are more aware and can make concrete reflections/suggestions.
Student surveys	Collect qualitative data from students about their perceptions and understanding of non-verbal feed-forward.
Student interviews	As above, but include specific open and closed questions to ask students about how non-verbal feed-forward helps them to identify the next steps in their learning.
Teacher appraisal	Including teacher interviews, how do teacher reflections suggest the level of impact non-verbal feed-forward is having on their workload, motivation, staff retention or engagement with professional development, or on behaviour and engagement in their class?
Lesson observation	Use video recordings of lessons to analyse and reflect on the use and impact of non-verbal feed-forward strategies in a range of curriculum subjects. Look for visible signs of students' understanding of, engagement in and response to these signals. How do these methods improve the quality of teaching across the school/college?
Case studies	Develop case studies in-house that focus on specific students or groups to determine whether they show any notable improvement in learning, behaviour, attendance or engagement. Attribute these changes to specific non-verbal feed-forward strategies. Compare how teachers adapt the ideas between different classrooms and how different students respond.
Subject take-up	As a result of any teacher using explicit non-verbal feed-forward strategies, is there an increase in students wanting to study their subject or wanting to be taught by this teacher?

There are many ways schools and colleges can evidence teachers' work in class. We need to move beyond everything being written down in students' exercise books as the main way of determining how teacher feedback impacts on student progress. This outdated concept needs to be put to bed!

- How does your school currently conduct scrutiny of students' work?
- What does this look like in subjects where there is more practical than written work?
- How could we – if at all – evaluate non-verbal language?

TEMPLATE

Quality assurance planning document

The template provided here is not simply a non-verbal feedback strategy template, but rather a planning document that you could use for quality assurance processes. The template should serve as a guide for you and school and college leaders to observe, record and reflect on the impact of the strategies that you use on various aspects of student learning.

Strategy evaluated	Non-verbal feed-forward	Attendance/ punctuality	Behaviour	Rewards and sanctions	Lesson observation	Student/ teacher interviews
Quality assurance method	To monitor the differences in student rewards and sanctions during the summer term.					
Description	This is an evaluation of strategies used in a Year [number] [subject] lesson during [time period], comparing one sample class and one control class for data collection. Student interviews will be conducted at the start and at the end of the trial period to determine what impact the strategy has had.					
Observations	Frequency of engagement Number of incidents Trends in data Comparison of rewards/sanctions Students' understanding of non-verbal feed-forward received Frequency of strategy used					

Strategy evaluated	Non-verbal feed-forward	Attendance/ punctuality	Behaviour	Rewards and sanctions	Lesson observation	Student/ teacher interviews
Evidence	Lesson observations Student interviews Reward data collection Sanction data collection Non-verbal feed-forward events in class					
Notes						

Scan to download a copy of the template

CHAPTER 10

WHAT NEXT?

In this chapter, I will summarise the **evolution of this book alongside the key findings and insights** I have discovered from each of the nine school and college case studies, as well as some of the research I have presented.

My original intention for writing this book stems back to my exploration into feedback, moving away from the preference favoured by school leaders and inspectors of having written feedback in exercise books to evidence progress.

Part of this exploration happened when I supported a group of 100+ teachers to document our teaching and learning thinking across three academic years. At the time, I was a deputy headteacher and this work culminated in publishing *Mark. Plan. Teach: Save Time, Reduce Workload, Impact Learning* (McGill, 2017). (There is now a second edition available, called *Mark. Plan. Teach. 2.0.*) We shared our work in teacher training sessions as we developed our teaching and learning policy. This policy became our song sheet, documenting our quality assurance processes and all the wider research and implementation frameworks in one place. I also shared that evolution on my blog, www.teachertoolkit.co.uk/blog.

I was frustrated with how our work at the time fell foul of poor quality assurance methods used by the inspectorate. The post-inspection adrenaline led me to research feedback further – notably verbal feedback. Why do some of the best system leaders fail to understand that you can evaluate progress without written commentary being evidenced? This culminated in a case study published with Mark Quinn and the University College London (McGill and Quinn, 2019), explained in Chapter 4, to understand how teachers grapple with written marking, particularly in disadvantaged schools, and how other forms of formative assessment manifest themselves in students' outcomes.

As a by-product of my experiences, research and day-to-day work, 'Mark, Plan, Teach' developed into a macro-consultation for schools and colleges everywhere. I would review their current teaching and learning policy during any initial consultation with the school leadership team. This led to understanding statutory and non-statutory guidance, developing a macro overview of what schools and colleges choose to value – a 'state of the nation' perspective. Several years later, I now have at least 500+ teaching and learning policies to hand. This book captures the latest chapter in my journey to help move the profession into the next decade.

EXPLAINER

Before I present my suggestions of how to implement all nine ideas inside the book – whether in your classroom or strategically across your organisation – I want to take a moment to share some other important work.

The Education Endowment Foundation's 'Feedback in action: A review of practice in English schools' (Elliott et al., 2020) is a detailed review of feedback practice across English schools. It provides evidence of feedback in action currently used in classrooms. The report 'triangulates documentary analysis of feedback policies, a medium-scale online survey of primary and secondary teachers, and in-depth interviews with teachers at eight case study institutions' (p. 16). It provides everyone with insights into what is currently happening in schools and how feedback is implemented. There is a useful overview of assessment for learning, professional development for teachers and supporting students with SEND. Some popular strategies, such as 'Directed Improvement and Reflection Time' (DIRT) and 'Feedback, Action, Response' (FAR) – a DIRT alternative – are also documented, because they provide teachers and students with practical methods for providing feedback and acting on feedback provided.

The report does, however, acknowledge that these insights are 'without evaluation of their effectiveness' (p. 16) and with 'limited empirical evidence' (p. 10) of the **implementation** of feedback within schools. Sadly, a simple linguistic analysis reveals the 145-page report only mentions 'feed-forward' twice, and 'feed-up' is not mentioned at all. But the word 'feedback' is mentioned over 1,000 times! We have much work to do with the dialogue of formative assessment if educational organisations are not pushing our thinking forward adequately.

While 'Feedback in action' is not a research paper, the Education Endowment Foundation did summarise their findings, calling for more research to understand the practical application of feedback in English classrooms, including a range of innovative practices.

Throughout this book, I have provided practical examples of how schools are implementing feedback in a range of ways to improve student outcomes and to reduce teacher workload and turnover and, more importantly, how we can evidence the traditional 'marking' and 'feedback' methods in a broader evidence base. My hope is that current and future teachers and leaders will use these practical examples to benefit the profession overall.

PRACTICAL IDEAS

Formative assessment identification

Before we evaluate the current techniques you are already using, scan the QR code below to map them all to gather a full perspective. This would be an excellent exercise to complete with your team or departmental members.

Scan to complete an evaluation exercise to see how many of the nine techniques you are using

How to use this resource

1. Write down some of the written marking ideas you currently use in Row 1 (**WRITTEN**).
2. Make a conscious effort to distinguish between some of the written techniques you use. For example, if you are providing students with a written grade or success criteria to help them, or if you map their recent performance against future predictions, then the strategy you are using is **written feed-up** (see Chapter 2).
3. Now, in Row 2 (**VERBAL**), think about the things you say to students. What type of assessment commentary do you give them? What scripts, methods or phrases do you use? Are you feeding back on how they have done? Are you signposting to them a comparison of their current moment in time to where they are (hopefully) going? Or are you explaining to them how to get to the next stage? For example, if you speak to students and explain to them what to do next, you are using **verbal feed-forward**.
4. For Row 2 (**VERBAL**), can you name three different verbal techniques? Do they have a pedagogical name you can refer back to?
5. Finally, in Row 3 (**NON-VERBAL**), if I gave you a 'thumbs up' to say 'you are nearly at the end!', based on how far you have read into this section of the book, where would you place my **non-verbal** gesture? Is this a feedback, a feed-up or a feed-forward strategy?

6. You (hopefully) will be left with nine different formative assessment ideas in your template – much like the nine case studies in this book.

Evaluating your current position

Your next challenge is to think about the strategic use of all nine methods and, more importantly, how you could quality-assure these techniques against student outcomes.

Next, let's think about all the techniques you currently use.

- Which are worth the effort?
- Which techniques do students respond to?
- Which techniques do students value more than others?
- What about parents? School and college leaders? Inspectors?
- Where should teachers focus their efforts so they can work more effectively, reducing their workload and adding significant value to students?
- How can teachers select ideas to work more efficiently?

'Teaching in the Green Zone' matrix

Use my 'Teaching in the Green Zone' matrix to determine what ideas are a waste of your time, versus which offer high impact for minimal effort.

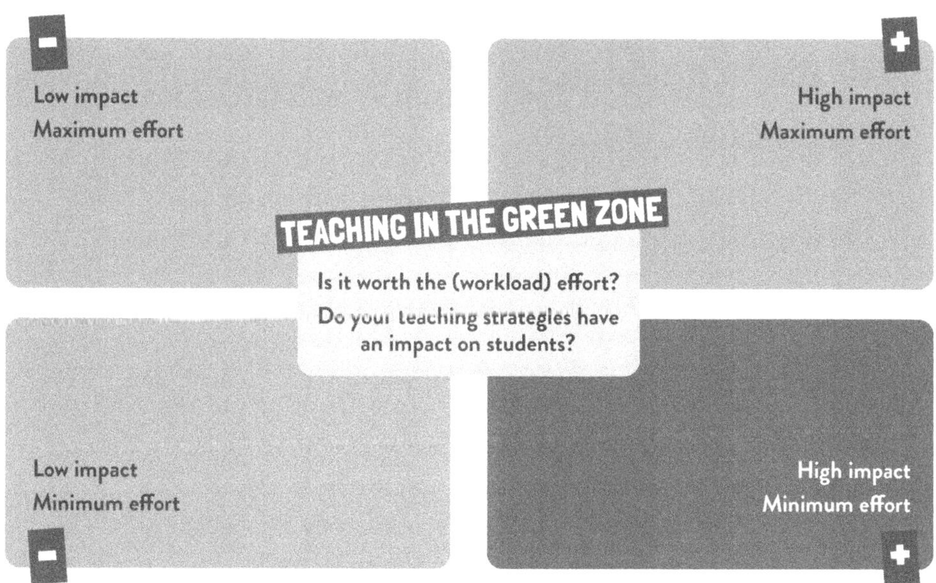

Scan for a digital version explanation of the 'Green Zone'

Note, this is not to say some ideas are worth abandoning altogether. It's to help you reflect on workload versus impact. Once complete, what could you do more or less of, to determine which techniques work best for different subjects, students and age groups?

Reflecting on organisational strategy

Below are three areas of practice grouped into beginner, intermediate and advanced levels. Each offers a range of suggestions that will align with some of the work your school or college is currently doing in your teaching and learning journey, policy and organisational priorities. (Note: Depending on your situation, the 'formative assessment CPD calendar' in the following chapter, 'Bringing it all together', can be used as an implementation plan to help guide your thinking forward.)

1. **Beginner**

   If your school or college still believes that written marking is the only way of sourcing feedback, then your school or classroom is likely to be at the 'beginner' stages of your feedback policy journey, especially if the following are **not embedded** in everyday practice:

   a. **Feedback framework:** Start by creating a simple, clear feedback policy that outlines the purpose, methods and expected outcomes of feedback in the classroom.

   b. **Staff training:** Organise professional development sessions on the basics, focusing on fundamental feedback techniques, including written, verbal and non-verbal methods, to ensure all staff are on the same page. Select the relevant chapter in this book and use the templates provided.

   c. **Start with small-scale implementation:** Use my 'Five-minute formative assessment plan' on page 130 to encourage school and college staff to incorporate basic classroom feedback strategies, such as thumbs up/down for quick checks or exit tickets for end-of-lesson reflections, and gradually build on these. Ask key team members to work in smaller groups so that everyone has a say in the formation of ideas as the implementation of your new policy evolves and then rolls out.

2. **Intermediate**

   Your school or classroom is likely to be at this 'intermediate' stage if you have some established practices that are familiar in this book, but recently, you are starting to understand new perspectives and approaches to formative assessment documented in this book. These ideas are for you if you are looking to deepen your teaching and learning effectiveness.

   a. **Refine your feedback methods:** Focus on diversifying feedback techniques, incorporating methods like verbal and non-verbal feedback, peer and self-assessment, including using digital tools for improving online feedback.

   b. **Consider how you may implement the practical examples in all nine chapters of this book:** How could you integrate the language of formative assessment into your current teaching and learning policy? Rather than 'marking' or 'feedback' scribbled throughout your current policy, change this to 'formative assessment', which includes all nine assessment variations highlighted by the case studies.

   c. **Feedback analysis:** Begin collecting and analysing feedback data to understand its impact on student learning, and use this data to refine practices. You will need to think very carefully about the processes you currently use and how these can evolve to consider other aspects of assessment cited throughout this book. Try using my **Formative Assessment Scorecard** (see page 124).

   d. **Collaborative strategies:** Promote collaborative feedback sessions where teachers can share and discuss their methods and experiences of any new ideas, fostering a culture of continuous development. For example, what does non-verbal feedback look like in a range of subjects, and how can each be valued by experts and non-specialist staff?

3. **Advanced**

   If you believe you are already carrying out the beginner and intermediate suggestions in your classroom, consider the more difficult question: How is this happening across all classrooms in your school and college, no matter what type of formative assessment is used between year groups or specialist subjects?

   If you are ready to consider moving up to the more 'advanced' stage of reflection, the following suggestions and techniques are offered as a 'test yourself' measure for schools, colleges, teachers and leaders who are already well versed in the nine 'feedback' strategies (see the Introduction) but are looking to pioneer new approaches that marry up with the one per cent of schools that I see who are already on this path. You may also want to test yourself against the influences created by Professor Rob Coe (see Introduction, on page xvi).

Here are some thought-provoking questions that can guide you on your journey:

1. Are you confident that all nine approaches can be/are used across your organisation?
2. Is there a coherent application of all nine *Teacher Toolkit Guide to Feedback* strategies across all year groups and subjects?
3. How do you ensure that every teacher uniformly understands and implements these approaches?
4. How does your leadership team actively support and model innovative formative assessment practices?
5. What role does governance play in championing these nine strategies across the organisation?
6. How are students involved in the development and evaluation of *Teacher Toolkit Guide to Feedback* strategies?
7. To what extent do your current methods empower students to take ownership of their learning journey?
8. What professional development opportunities are available for staff to further their understanding of *Teacher Toolkit Guide to Feedback* methods? Get in touch if you need help: **www.teachertoolkit.co.uk/training**
9. How do you systematically evaluate the impact of each strategy on student outcomes, engagement and teacher wellbeing? Use the **Formative Assessment Scorecard** to help with this (see page 124).
10. How is your school/college integrating technology to enhance these nine methods? For example, how do you ensure any retrieval practice software provides students with feedback, feed-up or feed-forward? Is the online tool only providing one type of feedback?
11. Are there untapped digital tools or platforms that could improve your approach to formative assessment? For example, video summaries of school reports for parents' evenings or video screengrabs of teachers providing formative assessment for students, all accessed by QR codes.

12. How does artificial intelligence feature in your teaching and learning policy (especially the formative assessment section)?
13. How do your current strategies adapt to meet the needs of all students, especially those with special educational needs or English as an additional language?
14. How regularly do you review your school/college feedback policy to ensure it aligns with the latest educational research and best practices? What evaluation method do you use?
15. What succession plan process is in place for adapting your teaching policy in response to new insights and evidence?
16. How do you ensure anyone conducting quality assurance in teacher classrooms is well versed in the nine strategies offered by *Teacher Toolkit Guide to Feedback*? How do observers draw upon a wide evidence base?
17. What emerging trends or research in education could influence your feedback practices? For example, in the field of neuroeducation, how does cognitive science and brain research influence how we teach, provide feedback and encourage students to take action?
18. How will you keep adopting and experimenting with cutting-edge feedback methods?

These questions encourage reflection, helping to advance teachers' CPD and school and college policy. If you believe you are already delivering all nine strategies in your classroom or across your organisation, or that this book has inspired your journey to take action, then I would love to hear from you! Email Support@TeacherToolkit.co.uk or tag @TeacherToolkit on social media.

Formative Assessment Scorecard

Depending on your role, the Formative Assessment Scorecard provides a structured approach to reflect and assess your current provision in the classroom or across the organisation.

1. As **teachers**, you can use this to reflect on how you approach different types of formative assessment in the classroom.
2. School and college **leaders** can use this to consider how they approach quality assurance, celebrating various ways to provide formative assessment.

3. School and college **governors** can use this to help curate a range of supportive and challenging questions for the leadership team. The matrix can be used to help equip governors with a wider understanding of assessment in classrooms, beyond just written marking!

Method	A. Currently used in the classroom (Yes/No)	B. Self-assessment (1 if used ad-hoc, 3 if used often)	C. How do you currently evaluate this method? (E.g. observations)	D. Where do you find these methods evident? (E.g. student books)	E. What teacher CPD is needed?
1. Written feedback					
2. Written feed-up					
3. Written feed-forward					
4. Verbal feedback					
5. Verbal feed-up					
6. Verbal feed-forward					
7. Non-verbal feedback					
8. Non-verbal feed-up					
9. Non-verbal feed-forward					
10. Total score:	Total column score One point for each Yes	Total column score	Calculate your overall score: Multiply 10A by 10B		

Scan to access a digital version of the formative assessment scorecard

Take a moment to reflect on the nine techniques and the five columns. This resource should be used as a personal reflection tool, as well as a whole-school training exercise. This mapping exercise is particularly useful if you believe you are in the 'intermediate' and 'advanced' stages of your feedback journey.

How to use this table

1. Start in Column A. Move down the page and indicate with a 'Yes' or a 'No' whether you currently use this technique explicitly in your classroom(s).
2. In Column B, if this idea is used frequently, is embedded within your practice and you have a range of examples to show how you would use this technique, then give yourself 3 points. If you have to double-think, you are likely a 1 or a 2, depending on your confidence level.
3. Total all the 'Yes' comments in Column A and give yourself one point for each (total of 9 points). Mark the total in row 10, Column A.
4. Total all the 1–3 points indicated in Column B, and add the total to row 10, Column B.
5. Take a moment to annotate your thoughts across rows 1–9, through Columns C–E. You will need at least five to ten minutes to complete this thoughtfully. Columns C and D will require some strategic thinking!
6. Just for a bit of fun, and at least to help you reflect on your journey, I have added a metric to row 10, Columns A–C to help you produce an overall final score.
7. Calculate your overall score found in row 10, Column A, multiplying that number by the number you have in row 10, Column B.
8. To see how you are currently doing, use the scoring criteria below:

- 0–81 points = Your formative assessment is currently at the same level as all school/college practice.
- 82–162 points = Your formative assessment is stronger than most.
- 163–243 points = Your formative assessment practice is cutting-edge!

Other possible questions that could be posed in Columns C–E include:

1. How embedded are the nine methods used in different subjects?
2. How embedded are the nine methods used with different age groups?
3. How are all nine methods shared with non-specialists, such as governors and families? For example, how do you help parents move forward with their perception that everything has to be marked?

Feedback Influence Scorecard

Now let's consider the influences at play when providing feedback. You and your colleagues may be 'champions at marking'! All your marking is up to date, teacher workload is managed, sometimes high, sometimes low, but there is no dialogue at teacher training level to factor in what influences are at work. We know that the most important aspect of good feedback is not how it is received but whether the student takes action. Currently, the work by the EEF features in most school teaching and learning policies: feedback must be manageable, meaningful and motivational. The phrase 'timely' also features in many school and college approaches. This langauge is dated from EEF publications printed in 2006.

In my next resource, I'd like you to scan the QR code to unlock a template and use the **Feedback Influence Scorecard** to evaluate the influences at play when providing feedback to your students. How do you factor these influences into your current quality assurance procedures?

Scan to use the Feedback Influence Scorecard

How to use this table

1. In a teacher training session or by yourself, note down a definition to match Rows 1–16.
2. In Column A, from Rows 1–16, score how well your school considers each 'influence' against your current school or college teaching and learning policy. For example, most organisations state that 'feedback should be timely' (see Row 8). If that is the case for you, give yourself a score of 2 (medium). It may be that, instead of giving immediate feedback, you and your workplace have made the conscious decision to delay feedback until a more suitable time within your curriculum. If that has been a genuine teacher CPD discussion in your work, score yourself a 3!
3. Work through all 16 rows, then state 'Yes' or 'No' in Column B for each influence. In column C, consider what training is needed for staff for the year ahead.

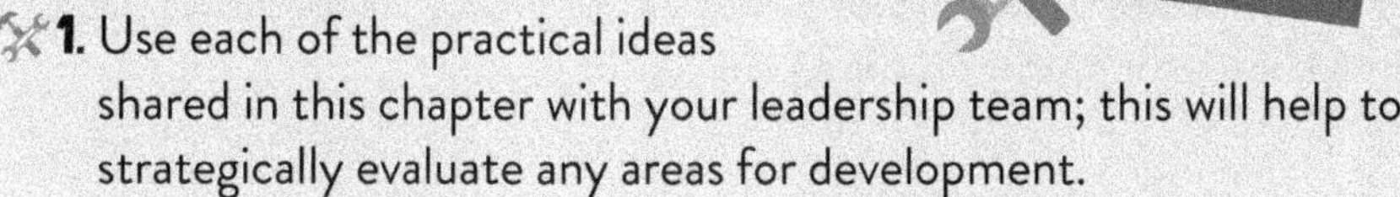

(For whole-school and college implementation)

1. Use each of the practical ideas shared in this chapter with your leadership team; this will help to strategically evaluate any areas for development.
2. Consider how students will interpret feedback, feed-up and feed-forward responses, and whether they are in written, verbal or non-verbal format. Factor SEND and neurodiverse students into your conversations and explore what good practice look like.
3. Reshape your current quality assurance processes (e.g. observations, work scrutiny) and consider how all forms of formative assessment can be monitored and evaluated. Think about the wider evidence base you could gather to demonstrate impact.
4. Ask your students! Design a structured questionnaire to gather student views; find out how they currently perceive all forms of formative assessment, what their preferences are and what may or may not work effectively.

WORKED EXAMPLE

Scan the QR code below for an example of how I would have completed the **formative assessment identification** document as a deputy headteacher of a large secondary school in London.

Scan to view an example of a completed formative assessment identification document

I have added some example techniques used in various classroom scenarios. You will be familiar with some of the techniques, but they might be called a different name. I've also included how I would evaluate some of the marking and feedback ideas, some of which are documented inside *Mark. Plan. Teach 2.0* (McGill, 2021), using the **Teaching in the Green Zone** matrix to evaluate which ideas are worth your effort.

Scan to view an example of using the 'Green Zone' matrix to evaluate ideas

These examples begin to showcase a comprehensive approach to evaluating and evidencing various formative assessment (feedback) methods, their application across different subjects and age groups, and how this information can be communicated to inspectors, governors and parents to improve overall teaching and learning.

TEMPLATE

Five-minute formative assessment plan

I want to provide you with my **Five-minute formative assessment plan**, which is a possible strategy of the practical steps a school or college could take if they want to take the recommendations of this book and place them as explicit techniques teachers should use on a month-by-month basis in their classrooms. Please use this as an example to inspire you, not as *the example* of how to do it.

Scan to access an exclusive five-minute plan for your current formative assessment work

You should also consider how this strategy would fit in with your current professional development programme, where you may or may not involve students, parents and governors, and how you might also adjust your teaching and learning policy in light of emerging findings.

BRINGING IT ALL TOGETHER

What should you do now?

In this final part of the book, I will share with you how to integrate the formative assessment methods that have been outlined in this book into your school or college classroom, to help influence your current teaching and learning policy and quality assurance methods. This should help broaden view when gathering a range of evidence to see how teachers' feedback impacts student progress.

Here is a reminder of the key messages from the Introduction:

1. moving away from 'marking' and 'feedback' phraseology
2. understanding both marking and feedback as formative assessment approaches
3. implementing nine ways to work with students
4. rethinking classroom evaluation
5. looking at how to support teacher workload.

Let's consider the nine case studies in the book, which cover a broad range of settings and which represent a snapshot of the teaching profession across England. I have shared with you how nine types of formative assessment methods – traditionally framed as 'marking' and 'feedback' – are implemented in real classroom settings. We've not even discussed questioning as a formative tool, but I can help you with this also – see *The Teacher Toolkit Guide To Questioning* (McGill, 2023).

A brief summary of all nine case studies

Each chapter has provided you with a tangible context in the classroom, illustrating how each of the nine feedback strategies have some practical application and impact. Here is a reminder of the fabulous work going on:

Chapter 1: Joseph Cash Primary School, Coventry – uses written feedback with Key Stage 2 students = they use the Orange Box method to provide detailed, actionable feedback to give students a clear focus and progress learning in small, manageable chunks. This is quality-assured and evidenced in written outcomes and student development.

Chapter 2: Dollis Primary School, London – uses written feed-up with Key Stage 1 students = they use a 'tackling the tricky bits' approach to cover key areas for improvement as a class and allow time for students to edit their work. This is quality-assured and evidenced in student participation in class.

Chapter 3: Waverley School, Birmingham – uses written feed-forward with Key Stage 2 students = they use a streamlined, whole-school feedback approach, including actionable feed-forward, which helps students to apply specific learning into future learning. This is quality-assured and evidenced in behaviour and attendance.

Chapter 4: Delta Independent School, County Durham – uses verbal feedback with Key Stage 3 and 4 students = they spend significant time getting to know each student and on CPD, to ensure that verbal feedback is tailored, constructive and positive; they find immediate verbal feedback helps pupil progress. This is quality-assured and evidenced in student engagement and attendance.

Chapter 5: Everton Free School, Liverpool – uses verbal feed-up with Key Stage 3 and 4 students = they use one-to-one verbal feed-up to assess each individual student's learning and offer praise to build their confidence. This is quality-assured and evidence in student ownership and self-regulation.

Chapter 6: Kennet School, Berkshire – uses verbal feed-forward with Key Stage 4 students = They use a 'live marking' approach, where teachers move around the classroom and help students with the steps required to move their work forward. This is quality-assured and evidenced in habitual behaviours and self-regulation in class.

Chapter 7: Withington Girls' School, Manchester – uses non-verbal feedback with Key Stage 3 and 4 students = they use non-verbal signals such as a thumbs-up to indicate to students how they are progressing without interrupting the flow of the lesson, giving students regular indications of how they are doing. This is quality-assured and evidenced in participation, confidence and metacognition in class.

Chapter 8: Leaways School, London – uses non-verbal feed-up with Key Stage 3 students = they use non-verbal cues to help students stay on task and maintain good behaviour in a non-confrontational manner, as well as to give students affirmation without interrupting the lesson flow. This is quality-assured and evidenced in engagement and behaviour.

Chapter 9: West London College, London – uses non-verbal feed-forward with Key Stage 5 students and adult learners = they use a 'signal, act, confirm' approach to signal to students what to focus on and offer them affirmation once they have acted on the focus, as well as a visual goal-setting approach to show students what to work on. This is quality-assured and evidenced in course retention and attendance.

What surprised me?

I was surprised how quickly the teachers from the school and college case studies replied to me to explain what they currently do. I was also impressed with how the nine ideas presented took their thinking one step forward. They involved colleagues and students in some initial observations, before responding with chapter contributions, video and audio examples and practical ideas. All nine schools will need to reflect on all nine methods going forward. This is also where you can help guide the future of the profession by assessing the impact of each of these nine methods. This assessment is key for improving the education system as a whole, particularly for student outcomes and teacher workload.

What should teachers do now?

You should now reflect on the overall teaching culture of your organisation. Involving parents, governors and students in this process is essential, but this must come after you and your school/college have done the hard thinking. To help you, encourage your school or college to take proactive steps in applying the knowledge and strategies discussed in this book. I suggest forming in-house collaborative CPD networks to share best practices and document a wide range of evidence. These could be captured in QR videos, where colleagues can see and hear other teachers working with your students, using these nine techniques. I will explain to you later in this chapter how I would organise a teacher training session – using this book to lead the implementation of all ideas in your classroom, school or college.

Formative Assessment Matrix

I have been inspired by the 'Matrix of feedback for learning' (Brooks et al., 2019) so, to help take your thinking one step forward, I have reconsidered how these feedback, feed-up and feed-forward strategies could be viewed when working with students who are either novice, intermediate or expert. What I have **not** done in this document is to differentiate the rows and columns by written, verbal or non-verbal methods.

Scan to download a completed example of the Formative Assessment Matrix to look over, plus a blank template to download and complete yourself

You could map out three written feedback, feed-up and feed-forward techniques, sub-divided into novice, intermediate and expert categories. During a reflection exercise of a CPD session with colleagues, you could identify what you use with your students. Then, do the same with verbal and non-verbal techniques.

The grid on the next page should inspire your thinking.

Written feedback	Written feed-up	Written feed-forward
Novice: What written feedback, feed-up and feed-forward techniques could you use to inspire your **novice students**?		
Intermediate: What written feedback, feed-up and feed-forward techniques could you use to inspire your **intermediate students**?		
Expert: What written feedback, feed-up and feed-forward techniques could you use to inspire your **expert students**?		

You should repeat this exercise by also reviewing the current verbal and non-verbal strategies you use. Again, differentiate the various levels of expertise your students currently have and vary the level of assessment you provide in return, according to their current ability and future progress.

How to design your own continuing professional development (CPD)

If we consider the academic year as nine months, we have nine formative assessment techniques in this book. Perfect! Now, I appreciate that not all schools and colleges will have the time set aside to focus on one particular aspect of this work, every month, when balancing all the other things that you have to manage. However, as I am always wanting to reach for the stars, perhaps you could think about how you could reshape or influence your school/college's professional development programme for the year ahead?

Nine ideas as a month-by-month resource

Here is an example of how to introduce each of the nine formative assessment techniques: (a) across your school or college and (b) in your classroom.

For example, when you first meet the class, one month into the new academic year you can use the techniques to motivate students and influence their future success. Provide verbal feed-forward to help explain to students what they should do next. This assessment would be immediate for students, reduce workload for you as a teacher and allow students to understand what action to take next. I have provided the calendar as an example to mirror three academic terms (summative assessment points) towards end-of-year examinations. The idea is that each strategy mirrors the academic year, progress in the classroom and teacher workload.

If you follow this QR code link, I show you how to put all the strategies together throughout an academic year so that they support and strengthen each other

Formative assessment CPD calendar

The formative assessment CPD calendar provides an example of whole-school/college professional development. Your organisation should consider how each technique could be introduced, developed or retrieved in monthly CPD sessions throughout the academic year. This CPD plan should mirror the techniques being used in classrooms as mapped out in the month-by-month resource above. (Note that the bulk of the work would be done between September and May, with June/July kept aside for round-up and tests.)

Introduce each technique month by month into your CPD calendar.

1. Discuss what the technique is.
2. What does it look like across subjects/key stages?
3. How would you evaluate this technique in quality control and assurance methods?

Each technique should be repositioned according to the curriculum being taught and the timeframe available.

September	October	November	December	January	February	March	April	May	June/July
Verbal Feed Forward A good way to provide early spoken guidance on future improvements.	**Written FeedBack** Retrospective comments, focusing on performance / areas to improve.	**Verbal Feed Up** A timely opportunity to remind students of targets and objectives.	**Non Verbal FeedBack** End of term visual cues to reinforce goals and expectations	**Verbal FeedBack** To provide immediate and early term spoken guidance on future improvements.	**Written Feed Forward** Advice on future tasks, guiding students how to apply feedback.	**Written Feed Up** Comments that help students align effort with their goals to clarify expectations.	**Non Verbal Feed Forward** Providing visual cues to students towards future actions and strategies.	**Non Verbal Feed Up** Pre-examination visual cues that reinforce learning goals and expectations.	
	Verbal Feed Forward A good way to provide early spoken guidance on future improvements.	**Written FeedBack** Retrospective comments, focusing on performance / areas to improve.	**Verbal Feed Up** A timely opportunity to remind students of targets and objectives.	**Non Verbal FeedBack** End of term visual cues to reinforce goals and expectations	**Verbal FeedBack** To provide immediate and early term spoken guidance on future improvements.	**Written Feed Forward** Advice on future tasks, guiding students how to apply feedback.	**Written Feed Up** Comments that help students align effort with their goals to clarify expectations.	**Non Verbal Feed Forward** Providing visual cues to students towards future actions and strategies.	**Non Verbal Feed Up** Pre-examination visual cues that reinforce learning goals and expectations.
		Verbal Feed Forward A good way to provide early spoken guidance on future improvements.	**Written FeedBack** Retrospective comments, focusing on performance / areas to improve.	**Verbal Feed Up** A timely opportunity to remind students of targets and objectives.	**Non Verbal FeedBack** End of term visual cues to reinforce goals and expectations	**Verbal FeedBack** To provide immediate and early term spoken guidance on future improvements.	**Written Feed Forward** Advice on future tasks, guiding students how to apply feedback.	**Written Feed Up** Comments that help students align effort with their goals to clarify expectations.	**Non Verbal Feed Forward** Providing visual cues to students towards future actions and strategies.
Introduce one new technique each month; deeper level each time			**Verbal Feed Forward** A good way to provide early spoken guidance on future improvements.	**Written FeedBack** Retrospective comments, focusing on performance / areas to improve.	**Verbal Feed Up** A timely opportunity to remind students of targets and objectives.	**Non Verbal FeedBack** End of term visual cues to reinforce goals and expectations	**Verbal FeedBack** To provide immediate and early term spoken guidance on future improvements.	**Written Feed Forward** Advice on future tasks, guiding students how to apply feedback.	**Written Feed Up** Comments that help students align effort with their goals to clarify expectations.
				Verbal Feed Forward A good way to provide early spoken guidance on future improvements.	**Written FeedBack** Retrospective comments, focusing on performance / areas to improve.	**Verbal Feed Up** A timely opportunity to remind students of targets and objectives.	**Non Verbal FeedBack** End of term visual cues to reinforce goals and expectations	**Verbal FeedBack** To provide immediate and early term spoken guidance on future improvements.	**Written Feed Forward** Advice on future tasks, guiding students how to apply feedback.
					Verbal Feed Forward A good way to provide early spoken guidance on future improvements.	**Written FeedBack** Retrospective comments, focusing on performance / areas to improve.	**Verbal Feed Up** A timely opportunity to remind students of targets and objectives.	**Non Verbal FeedBack** End of term visual cues to reinforce goals and expectations	**Verbal FeedBack** To provide immediate and early term spoken guidance on future improvements.
						Verbal Feed Forward A good way to provide early spoken guidance on future improvements.	**Written FeedBack** Retrospective comments, focusing on performance / areas to improve.	**Verbal Feed Up** A timely opportunity to remind students of targets and objectives.	**Non Verbal FeedBack** End of term visual cues to reinforce goals and expectations
							Verbal Feed Forward A good way to provide early spoken guidance on future improvements.	**Written FeedBack** Retrospective comments, focusing on performance / areas to improve.	**Verbal Feed Up** A timely opportunity to remind students of targets and objectives.
									Written FeedBack Retrospective comments, focusing on performance / areas to improve.

Scan to download a digital template of the CPD calendar

This calendar is designed to match the rhythm of the academic year, so I have considered the placement of each of the nine techniques to suit the year. This is where we, as teachers, would expect students to progress, in keeping with summative assessments taking place throughout the year. However, remember that context is key. What you would do in a school or college where students are predominantly visually or hearing-impaired will be very different to a mainstream school or college.

Remember, the resource included in the above QR code is an example. You will need to modify my version to suit your subject and the age group of students you teach. For example, you may have more than one strategy in one month, or you might just use one strategy each term. In the example I provided, I've tried to think about using all nine techniques to reduce the written burden on teachers, but also to fit in with the rhythm of most schools' summative assessment calendar.

CONCLUSION

Research

The Verbal Feedback Project (2019) research with Mark Quinn, commissioned by University College London, was a significant milestone in this book's journey. This research, for the first time, provided case study evidence from challenging state schools across England. It demonstrated that when a group of teachers provided verbal feedback instead of written, it made a tangible difference to students. My hope for this book is that we take the dialogue of marking and feedback into a new era, so that the burden of marking, or the wider perception of feedback, does not continue to penalise teachers or exacerbate workload.

Limitations

As with all academic research, there are limitations to research studies. This is no different to the work I have conducted in this book. There are only nine schools and colleges represented here – a small sample of the 20,000+ organisations across England. I am also confident that there will be more than nine techniques identified once this book is published, based on your response to the ideas inside and how you take them forward. Please keep me informed by tagging me on social media with the hashtag: #GuideToFeedback

Final reflections

I'm very impressed with how the schools mentioned in this book responded to my challenge about how they would provide a range of techniques and evidence to match one of the nine strategies explained in this book. I hope that this book becomes the catalyst for your journey, at whatever stage you are, and ultimately, I hope that it contributes to a wider discussion on marking and feedback across the profession.

Taking these ideas forward

At the time of writing, we we don't yet know the true impact of artificial intelligence (AI) and what this looks like in practice. We had some ideas that algorithms, computers and chat boxes would control or support the things that we do. Across every industry, including education, AI has already shaped many teaching and learning policies, factoring in plagiarism, copyright, referencing and content generation, particularly for students when submitting work. It has been fascinating to see how quickly this trend has influenced all aspects of life and how it has rippled down into our classrooms. It's still early days, but I do wonder how AI will influence feedback provided by teachers for students? Will students be able to trust the feedback, knowing that it has been artificially generated? After all, the dialogue of feedback has been actively evolving for several decades, so whoever uses it can only act upon feedback received, based on what is already known. Therefore, the feedback generated may not be something a student will necessarily understand, as there will be no human there in that moment to help the student translate it and take action.

How will the nine techniques explained in this book influence you in the modern world? You may need to adapt your feedback approaches in light of AI, to accommodate the significant growth in social media, young people's mental health issues and worsening local authority services. We all need some form of 'feedback' to motivate us, in all aspects of life, particularly in things we are learning to do, in or out of school. We know that feedback can support our wellbeing, motivations and future aspirations. How teachers do this in or out of the 'classroom of the future' will challenge those who work on the front line.

It has taken me several years to reach this stage in my pedagogy. I hope that by documenting it here, I can help you and many other teachers to go one step further to make teaching even more efficient and effective.

On my travels, I see so much brilliance in classrooms throughout the country. My wish is that *The Teacher Toolkit Guide to Feedback* influences the teaching and learning culture in your school/college, and that I have played a small part in your journey too. Once you have read this book, please recommend it to another colleague so that our 'feedback revolution' can ripple on further.

REFERENCES

Ahuja, S. (2010). Role of non verbal communication in improving quality of teaching learning process. In: S. Kumar and S. Srivastava, eds., *School Education in India: Quality Improvement Techniques*. New Delhi: New Century Publications, Chapter 6.

Allen, R., Benhenda, A., Jerrim, J. and Sims, S. (2020). New evidence on teachers' working hours in England: An empirical analysis of four datasets. *Research Papers in Education*, 36(6), pp. 1–25.

Andersen, J.F. and Andersen, P.A. (1987). Never smile until Christmas? Casting doubt on an old myth. *Journal of Thought*, 22(4), pp. 57–61.

Anderson, C.J. (2012). Feed-up, feedback and feedforward: Re-examining effective teacher–student interaction. In: *Perfect Score: Methodologies, Technologies, & Communities of Practice*. [online] Proceedings of the 20th Annual KOTESOL International Conference, Seoul, Korea. Available at: www.koreatesol.org/sites/default/files/pdf_publications/KOTESOL-Proceeds2012web.pdf#page=186 [Accessed 18 Apr. 2024].

Arnold, M. (2020). Giving students a chance to learn: Hitting pause and engaging students. *Journal on Empowering Teaching Excellence*, [online] 4(2). doi: https://doi.org/10.26077/fead-b454.

Black, P. and Wiliam, D. (1998a). *Inside the Black Box: Raising Standards through Classroom Assessment*. Cheltenham, Vic.: Hawker Brownlow Education.

Black, P. and Wiliam, D. (1998b). Assessment and classroom learning. *Assessment in Education: Principles, Policy & Practice*, 5(1), pp. 7–74.

Black, P. and Wiliam, D. (2006). Developing a theory of formative assessment. In J. Gardner (Ed.), *Assessment and Learning*, pp. 81–100. London: Sage.

Boon, S.I. (2016). Increasing the uptake of peer feedback in primary school writing: Findings from an action research enquiry. *Education 3-13*, 44(2), pp. 212–225.

British Deaf Association (2012). *BSL Strategy (2nd edition): Transforming Deaf People's Lives*. [online] pp. 1–28. Available at: https://bda.org.uk/wp-content/uploads/2017/03/Transforming-Deaf-Lives-contents.pdf%C2%A0 [Accessed 21 Apr. 2024].

British Deaf Association (n.d.). *What is BSL?* [online] Available at: https://bda.org.uk/help-resources [Accessed 15 Jul. 2024].

Brooks, C., Carroll, A., Gillies, R.M. and Hattie, J. (2019). A matrix of feedback for learning. *Australian Journal of Teacher Education*, [online] 44(4). Available at: https://files.eric.ed.gov/fulltext/EJ1213749.pdf [Accessed 18 Apr. 2024].

Carmody, R. (2019). Using student goal setting and feedback to encourage independent learning. *Australian Art Education*, 40(1), pp. 135–154.

Chan, S. and Leijten, F. (2014). Using feedback strategies to improve peer-learning in welding. *International Journal of Training Research*, 10(1), pp.23–29.

Coe, R. (2006). Can feedback improve teaching? A review of the social science literature with a view to identifying the conditions under which giving feedback to teachers will result in improved performance. *Research Papers in Education*, 13(1), pp. 43–66.

Coe, R. (2013). *Improving education: A triumph of hope over experience.* [online] Available at: http://eachandeverydog.net/wp-content/uploads/2015/05/ImprovingEducation2013.pdf [Accessed 9 May 2024].

Consortium for Research in Deaf Education (2023). *CRIDE 2023 England Report* [online] Available at: https://www.ndcs.org.uk/information-and-support/professionals/research-and-data/cride-reports/ [Accessed 21 Apr. 2024].

Couper, L. (2015). *The communication choices of students with autism spectrum disorder who are nonverbal.* [Thesis] [online] Available at: https://ir.canterbury.ac.nz/server/api/core/bitstreams/e33684de-a015-43ac-8b12-cc2edf872c5a/content [Accessed 21 Apr. 2024].

Department for Education (2016). *Reducing teacher workload: Marking Policy Review Group report.* [online] pp. 1–13. Available at: https://assets.publishing.service.gov.uk/media/5a75129f40f0b6360e47322f/Eliminating-unnecessary-workload-around-marking.pdf [Accessed 18 Apr. 2024].

Department for Education (2018). *School workload reduction toolkit.* [online] Available at: www.gov.uk/guidance/school-workload-reduction-toolkit [Accessed 18 Apr. 2024].

Department for Education (2019). *Early career framework.* [online] Available at: https://assets.publishing.service.gov.uk/media/60795936d3bf7f400b462d74/Early-Career_Framework_April_2021.pdf [Accessed 24 Jul. 2024].

Department for Education (2023a). *Working lives of teachers and leaders – wave 1: Research report.* [online] Available at: https://assets.publishing.service.gov.uk/government/uploads/system/uploads/attachment_data/file/1148571/Working_lives_of_teachers_and_leaders_-_wave_1_-_core_report.pdf [Accessed 9 May 2024].

Department for Education (2023b). British Sign Language GCSE: Everything you need to know. *The Education Hub.* [online] Available at: https://educationhub.blog.gov.uk/2023/12/21/british-sign-language-gcse-everything-you-need-to-know [Accessed 21 Apr. 2024].

Department for Education (2024). *Improve workload and wellbeing for school staff.* [online] Available at: www.gov.uk/guidance/improve-workload-and-wellbeing-for-school-staff [Accessed 9 May 2024].

Duncan, N. (2007). 'Feed-forward': Improving students' use of tutors' comments. *Assessment & Evaluation in Higher Education*, 32(3), pp. 271–283.

Dushkin, A.M. (1932). The Jewish educational system – a plea for organic unity. *Jewish Education*, 4(2), pp. 76–80.

Education Endowment Foundation (2021). *Teacher feedback to improve pupil learning: Guidance report.* [online] Available at: https://educationendowmentfoundation.org.uk/education-evidence/guidance-reports/feedback [Accessed 18 Apr. 2024].

Elliott, V., Baird, J.-A., Hopfenzbeck, T.N., Ingram, J., Thompson, I., Usher, N., Zantout, M., Richardson, J. and Coleman, R. (2016). *A marked improvement? A review of the evidence on written marking.* [online] Education Endowment Foundation. Available at: https://educationendowmentfoundation.org.uk/education-evidence/evidence-reviews/written-marking [Accessed 22 Apr. 2024].

Elliott, V., Randhawa, A., Ingram, J., Nelson-Addy, L., Griffin, C. and Baird, J.A. (2020). *Feedback in action: A review of practice in English schools.* [online] Education Endowment Foundation. Available at: https://ora.ox.ac.uk/objects/uuid:6c8ad1dd-e6ce-4f0a-9f7edd17140247e4/download_file?file_format=application%2Fpdf&safe_filename=Elliott_et_al_2020_Feedback_in_action_.pdf&type_of_work=Report&utm_source=pocket_saves [Accessed 25 Jul. 2024]

Ellis, N.J. and Loughland, T. (2017). 'Where to next?' Examining feedback received by teacher education students. *Issues in Educational Research*, 27(1), pp. 51–63.

Eriksson, E. (2021). Constructing clarity – Swedish teachers' and students' shared concern in feedback interaction in primary school classrooms. *Education 3-13*, 51(1), pp. 13–25.

Hardman, W. and Bell, H. (2017). 'More fronted adverbials than ever before': Writing feedback practices and grammatical metalanguage in an English primary school. *Language and Education*, 33(1), pp. 35–50.

Hattie, J. (2009). *Visible Learning: A Synthesis of Over 800 Meta-Analyses Relating to Achievement.* London: Routledge.

Hattie, J. and Timperley, H. (2007). The power of feedback. *Review of Educational Research*, 77(1), pp. 81–112.

John, O., Naumann, L.P. and Soto, C.J. (2008). Paradigm shift to the integrative big five trait taxonomy: History, measurement, and conceptual issues. In: O.P. John, R.W. Robins and L.A. Pervin, eds., *Handbook of Personality: Theory and Research*. New York: Guilford Press, pp. 114–158.

Kerr, K. (2017). Exploring student perceptions of verbal feedback. *Research Papers in Education*, 32(4), pp. 444–462.

Kluger, A.N. and DeNisi, A. (1996). The effects of feedback interventions on performance: A historical review, a meta-analysis, and a preliminary feedback intervention theory. *Psychological Bulletin*, 119(2), pp. 254–284.

Koen, M., Bitzer, E.M. and Beets, P.A.D. (2012). Feedback or feed-forward? A case study in one higher education classroom. *Journal of Social Sciences*, 32(2), pp. 231–242.

Lindner, J. (2017). *The art of good feedback: Training for effective peer feedback.* [online] Science Shop, University of Groningen. Available at: www.rug.nl/society-business/science-shops/taal-cultuur-en-communicatie/projecten/3-publicaties-en-rapporten/1708-training-voor-effectieve-peerfeedback-en.pdf [Accessed 18 Apr. 2024].

Malik, S. (2023). A study on the impact of non-verbal communication of secondary teachers on their classroom students. *Lingaya's Lalita Devi Journal of Professional Studies*, 8(9), pp. 28–39.

Mandouit, L. and Hattie, J. (2023). Revisiting 'The Power of Feedback' from the perspective of the learner. *Learning and Instruction*, [online] 84. doi: https://doi.org/10.1016/j.learninstruc.2022.101718.

McGill, R.M. (2017). *Mark. Plan. Teach: Save Time, Reduce Workload, Impact Learning*. 1st ed. London: Bloomsbury Education.

McGill, R.M. (2021). *Mark. Plan. Teach 2.0*. 2nd ed. London: Bloomsbury Education.

McGill, R.M. (2022). *The Teacher Toolkit Guide to Memory*. London: Bloomsbury Education.

McGill, R.M. (2023). *The Teacher Toolkit Guide to Questioning*. London: Bloomsbury Education.

McGill, R.M. and Quinn, M. (2019). *UCL Verbal Feedback Project report 2019*. [online] UCL. Available at: https://discovery.ucl.ac.uk/id/eprint/10111936/1/2019_verbal_feedback_project_final_4_print.pdf [Accessed 18 Apr. 2024].

Miller, P.W. (1986). *Nonverbal Communication (What Research Says to the Teacher)*. 2nd ed. Washington, D.C.: National Education Association.

Moir, T. (2023). *How to Create Autonomous Learners: Teaching Metacognitive, Self-Regulatory and Study Skills – a Practitioner's Guide*. Abingdon: Routledge.

Murphy, K. and Barry, S. (2015). Feed-forward: Students gaining more from assessment via deeper engagement in video-recorded presentations. *Assessment and Evaluation in Higher Education*, 41(2), pp. 213–227.

Nicol, D.J. and Macfarlane-Dick, D. (2006). Formative assessment and self-regulated learning: A model and seven principles of good feedback practice. *Studies in Higher Education*, 31(2), pp. 199–218.

Nuthall, G. (2001). *The cultural myths and the realities of teaching and learning*. [online] Available at: www.teachertoolkit.co.uk/wp-content/uploads/2018/05/Graham_Nuthall_2001.pdf [Accessed 21 Apr. 2024].

Orsmond, P., Maw, S.J., Park, J.R., Gomez, S. and Crook, A.C. (2011). Moving feedback forward: Theory to practice. *Assessment and Evaluation in Higher Education*, 38(2), pp. 240–252.

Pollari, P. (2017). To feed back or to feed forward? Students' experiences of and responses to feedback in a Finnish EFL classroom. *Apples – Journal of Applied Language Studies*, 11(4), pp. 11–33.

Roby, Y. (2022). *Teachers' written feedback in English: How does this relate to the pathways leading to self-regulated learning in 11–13 year old students.* [Dissertation] [online] Available at: https://ora.ox.ac.uk/objects/uuid:ddc34e70-ec74-492f-a45c-7270ac996f6f/download_file?file_format=application%2Fpdf&safe_filename=Roby_2022_Teachers_written_feedback.pdf&type_of_work=Thesis [Accessed 18 Apr. 2024].

Ruelmann, M., Charalambous, C.Y. and Praetorius, A.-K. (2022). The representation of feedback literature in classroom observation frameworks: An exploratory study. *Educational Assessment, Evaluation and Accountability*, 35, pp. 67–104.

Rust, C., Price, M. and O'Donovan, B. (2010). Improving students' learning by developing their understanding of assessment criteria and processes. *Assessment and Evaluation in Higher Education*, 28(2), pp. 147–164.

Sadler, D.R. (1989). Formative assessment and the design of instructional systems. *Instructional Science*, 18(2), pp. 119–144.

Soderstrom, N.C. and Bjork, R.A. (2015). Learning versus performance: An integrative review. *Perspectives on Psychological Science*, 10(2), pp. 176–199.

Stefanakis, E.H. (2002). *Multiple Intelligences and Portfolios: A Window into the Learner's Mind*. Portsmouth, N.H.: Heinemann.

Swinson, J. and Knight, R. (2007). Teacher verbal feedback directed towards secondary pupils with challenging behaviour and its relationship to their behaviour. *Educational Psychology in Practice*, 23(3), pp. 241–255.

Teacher Tapp (2019). *Marking matters (or does it)?* [online] Available at: https://teachertapp.co.uk/articles/marking-matters-or-does-it [Accessed 19 Apr. 2024].

Teacher Tapp (2022). *What are the reasons for dreading classes and how does your school's marking policy differ? This, and more...* [online] Available at: https://teachertapp.co.uk/articles/what-are-the-reasons-for-dreading-classes-and-how-does-your-schools-marking-policy-differ-this-and-more [Accessed 18 Apr. 2024].

@TeacherToolkit (n.d.). *Latest blog posts*. [online] Available at: www.teachertoolkit.co.uk/blog [Accessed 22 Apr. 2024].

Wimshurst, K. and Manning, M. (2012). Feed-forward assessment, exemplars and peer marking: Evidence of efficacy. *Assessment & Evaluation in Higher Education*, 38(4), pp. 451–465.

Wisniewski, B., Zierer, K. and Hattie, J. (2020). The power of feedback revisited: A meta-analysis of educational feedback research. *Frontiers in Psychology*, [online] 10. doi: https://doi.org/10.3389/fpsyg.2019.03087.

Zahorik, J.A. (1967). The nature and value of teacher verbal feedback. *ERIC*. [online] Available at: https://files.eric.ed.gov/fulltext/ED011526.pdf [Accessed 19 Apr. 2024].

Zarrinabadi, N. and Rezazadeh, M. (2023). Why only feedback? Including feed up and feed forward improves non-linguistic aspects of L2 writing. *Language Teaching Research*, [online] 27(3). doi: https://doi.org/10.1177/1362168820960725.

INDEX

G

H

I

J

K

L

M

N

O

P

Q

R

S

T

V

W

OTHER TITLES BY ROSS MORRISON McGILL

100 Ideas for Secondary Teachers: Outstanding Lessons
Just Great Teaching
Mark. Plan. Teach. 2.0
Teacher Toolkit

If you want to read more from this series...

THE TEACHER TOOLKIT GUIDE TO QUESTIONING

From Ross Morrison McGill, bestselling author of *Mark. Plan. Teach.* and *Teacher Toolkit*, this book highlights the importance of questioning in challenging pupils, checking for understanding, identifying gaps in knowledge, improving recall and ultimately encouraging learners to analyse, evaluate and actively engage in learning.

By simplifying the theory and offering original ideas proven to have an impact in the classroom, *The Teacher Toolkit Guide to Questioning* provides teachers with an invaluable resource to refine this key element of their practice.

The Teacher Toolkit Guide to Questioning was Highly Commended in the Assessment category at the Teach Secondary Awards 2023.

'It's Ross's best one yet! What a fantastic read.'
Libby Isaac, deputy head

'Every educator should own a copy of this book.'
Sarah Lewtas, primary teacher

Available to purchase at www.bloomsbury.com/uk, where you can also view an extract from inside the book!

ABOUT THE AUTHOR

Ross is known globally as @TeacherToolkit. To date, over 19 million people have read his website! He began teaching in 1991 and taught design and technology for 26 years in some of London's most challenging secondary schools, with 20 years as a school leader. In 2015, he was nominated as one of the '500 most influential people in Britain' by *The Sunday Times* and remains the only classroom teacher to feature to this day. Today, he works with students, teachers and school leaders worldwide, enhancing teaching and learning, workload and teacher mental health.

As one of the most followed educators globally on social media, Ross offers unique social media insights and support for teachers, schools and organisations. He is frequently asked to speak at national conferences and has worked with over 100,000 teachers worldwide. He is regularly asked to reflect on educational developments in multiple publications about education policy, championing the brilliance of teaching and unpacking the complexity of the classroom. Ross is also a PGCE tutor and visiting lecturer at the University of Buckingham, and when he is not researching, he is usually teaching teachers, creating resources or posting content as @TeacherToolkit! Ross is the bestselling author of *Mark. Plan. Teach. 2.0*, *Teacher Toolkit: Just Great Teaching*, *The Teacher Toolkit Guide to Memory* and *The Teacher Toolkit Guide to Questioning*.